# MY LOVE
## *to you*
# ALWAYS

Blessings for you Second Chances!

Suzanne Reeves

# MY LOVE *to you* ALWAYS

## 42 REAL STORIES OF ENDURING LOVE

COMPILED & EDITED BY
RAMONA TUCKER & JENNIFER WESSNER

OAKTARA

Waterford, Virginia

*My Love to You Always*

Published in the U.S. by:
**OakTara Publishers,** P.O. Box 8, Waterford, VA 20197
**www.oaktara.com**

Cover design by Yvonne Parks at www.pearcreative.ca
Cover images © thinkstockphotos.ca: couple holding hands/Jupiter Images;
shutterstock.com: road and perfect sunset sky/Iakov Kalinin

ISBN: 978-1-60290-336-4

Printed in the U.S.A.

# Contents

\* \* \*

# My Love to You Always

* * *

## INTRODUCTION

Love is like friendship caught on fire.
In the beginning a flame, very pretty, often hot and fierce,
but still only light and flickering.
As love grows older, our hearts mature
and our love becomes as coals,
deep-burning and unquenchable.
—BRUCE LEE

Love is a friendship set to music.
—E. JOSEPH COSSMAN

When did you begin your journey of love with your loved one? How have you kept your romance going, in the midst of life's challenges? In what ways have you learned to love always and develop a love that lasts for a lifetime? And if you've loved and lost, how have you found the courage to love again?

Nestled in this treasured volume are 42 of the best-of-the-best "lasting love" stories from our international search for sweet, real-life love stories. They're guaranteed to make you misty-eyed, renew your faith in love and magical moments, and to give you courage, hope, and joy as you follow life's path with your loved ones.

# A Welcome Interruption

* * *

## JESSICA KELLER

Crumpled papers carpet the ground as I pluck away at the keyboard, my eyes strained from too many late nights in front of this glowing monitor. The purple, fuzzy alarm clock I placed in the office for those times when I have to nap glares that it's midnight. Ah. That's right. Welcome to the sweet life of a college newspaper editor the week before finals.

The sound of undergraduates celebrating in the student center floats through the vents. If only. My rejoicing can't begin until the editing and layout is done, and the nonfiction narrative for my class is written, and I still have to finish reading the last chapter of a book. Who am I kidding? I'm also a resident assistant and need to close down the dorm before winter break, so jubilee won't be served on my plate until it saddles up next to the turkey at Christmas dinner.

I turn my head, scowling at the ringing phone. There is no reason, no reason at all, for anyone to call the newspaper office at this hour on a Wednesday night. There's no way I'm answering it, probably just some underclassman trying to prank me. But then on the other hand it could possibly be someone calling with a tip or idea that I should squeeze in last minute. The paper could use a lift, especially this addition which I fear will be used to wrap more presents than read. Ugh. Fine. The public wins. Snapping the receiver up in my hands, I answer.

"Jess? Is that you?" I recognize my boyfriend, Matt, by his distinct deep voice immediately.

Matt and I have been dating since the end of Freshman year, so by now, halfway through our Senior year, we're comfortable with each other. I'm proud of the man I'm dating; he's everything I could hope for. He loves the Lord, he's focused, he's over six-feet tall, and just so happens to have Prince Charming good looks. Which is all fine and well, but I don't want to talk to him right now. See, he's an extrovert and will keep me on the line for the next hour, and he knows that I'm an introvert and don't want to be bothered while

I'm in my editor's cave.

So I give a curt. "Need something?"

"Come out with me."

"I can't. There is no way. I still have the bulk of the newspaper to go, and let's not mention all the finals stuff I haven't started working on."

"Please. I haven't seen you all week."

"'Cause I've been busy all week…let's grab lunch together tomorrow."

"But I want to see you now." Oh. He has that soft sincere longing in his voice that's difficult to resist.

"Now? I've got a lot of stuff to do."

"You said that. Live a little, Jess."

He always gets me with the "live a little" part. A good time to me usually includes my pjs, the ratty yellow wingback chair I lugged to college from my parent's home, and a good novel. I'd probably end up happily living the life of a hermit on Walden Pond if it wasn't for Matt's occasional benevolent admonishing.

Not one to be bested, I rise to his challenge. "Fine. Where do you want to meet?"

"I'm outside; the car's warm already." The rat! He would have the gall to assume.

Hanging up the phone, I toe into black wool boots and yank a red puffy jacket over the too-large college sweater I shrugged into earlier that night. No makeup. I pull on a pink winter cap and sling the green striped scarf around my neck. It's the kind of outfit that can make a small child start crying, but I didn't think I'd see anyone tonight. At least it's dark.

Tromping through the two feet of snow God had recently decided to bless Chicago with, I make it to the car and sit down.

Matt's face lights up, and I catch my breath. How does he do that? He gets even more handsome with just a small gesture.

He throws the car into reverse. "Sexy get-up."

"Thanks. I try."

We spend the ride catching up, sharing stories from the week since we've been too swamped with schoolwork to cross paths. I tell him about the girls on my floor who decided to make a music video at three in the morning two nights ago. He laughs and tells me about his internship.

Then I tune in to my surroundings. He's driving towards the lake. "Where are you taking me? Matt? I really can't be gone long."

During the spring and autumn, we frequent Lake Michigan and walk hand-in-hand up the shore, but its winter in the Windy City, which equals

4

blasts of freezing air that are multiplied tenfold near the water.

He doesn't answer right away. Instead, he rounds the car and opens my door, ushering me out into the chill. His arm instinctively wraps around my shoulders as mine snakes around his middle. We fit. And despite the coldness outside, I feel warm.

Sliding down the ice-laden stairs I gasp down deep breaths of refreshing air, which puff out, sending tiny clouds heavenward. "You're crazy. You know that, right?" I tilt my face up to see his. He just smiles.

We arrive at the beach and, as we look around, a tingle of excitement races down my spine because the snow is completely untouched. No one else had stepped here since the snow fell four days ago. An expanse of moon-splashed whiteness glitters at our feet. It's pristine, and it almost hurts to ruin it. But that feeling passes quickly.

Taking off at a soccer-paced run I leave Matt in my powdery dust. A rush of exhilaration surges through my blood as I hear him trudging closer. His legs are much longer, so he catches up quickly and tackles me as we both shake with laugher. Covered, we giggle, brushing snow off each other's face.

Matt springs up, offering his hand. I take it, and if feels like home. Palm to palm, we walk nearer to the lake. The sound of cracking ice bounces off the barrier rocks and echoes in the hollow of trees at the edge of the beach. The lake is reckless, spitting its tide up above the thin winter layer.

And as I look out, the slow lapping of the water eases the tension left in my body. Finals are forgotten. The newspaper is forgotten. The cold isn't even acknowledged. My only realization is that I'm in the middle of the most beautiful moment I've ever experienced and it's all because of my best friend, my boyfriend, the love of my life.

Wait. Love of my life? I shake loose of his hold and pace a few feet away. Sure. We've been dating for almost three years now, but we're slow movers. Our entire relationship has been focused on building a solid friendship and knowing each other. There has been no love declarations, no kiss. We've both promised to wait until we know it's the person we are going to marry.

I gulp audibly.

I want to kiss him. I know, right in this moment, with my frostbitten toes and stress bubbling just below the surface, this is the man I want to spend the rest of my life with. Just an arm's length away stands the answers to my prayers for a godly husband, for a man who will make me laugh, and who knows what I need more than I do.

I feel Matt's hand on my shoulder as he turns me to face him. In the light of the silvery moon, he bends down and our lips meet in a kiss that gently baptizes me with his love.

And now, after five years of marriage, I still think back on that night with a sigh.

I'm so glad I picked up the phone.

JESSICA KELLER has had three articles published in the magazine *Encounters* (Standard Press), two short stories in their anthology *Encounters With God,* and a novella *The Potential of Kitty Bennet* in the anthology *The Road to Pemberley* (Ulysses Press). Her debut novel will release in February 2013.

**http://JessAWorkInProgress.blogspot.com**

# Love Always...

## * * *

### HOLLY BLEVINS

My love story began long before I knew it. God had begun to move every puzzle piece exactly into place, although to me, the picture seemed doomed to failure. At age 16, having had quite a few years of rebellion under my belt, I (begrudgingly) moved with my family from Florida to a quaint little town in Virginia called Ashburn. Surrounded by seemingly endless cornfields, there was nothing to do except venture to the 24-hour Walmart or attend church. My mother was in favor of church, so after weeks of boredom I was willing to humor her and try it out. We found a local youth group where I was welcomed with open arms. I learned that my troubled past was no longer a prediction of my future and, within a few months, I dedicated my life to Jesus. All that I had given away and all that had been lost in my young life was restored to me through Christ. I quickly became an integral part of the ministry team. I poured myself into learning what the Bible said and applying it to my life.

Halfway through that first year, after leading worship on a Wednesday night, I met Jay Blevins. He waited for the right time and confidently approached me. I'll never forget the first words he spoke to me: "Do you want a piece of gum?"

Not exactly words to melt a girl's heart, but they were so sincere. As we started spending more time together, it was always his sincerity that shined through. He was the opposite of every boy I had ever dated. He was strong, funny, and honest. Although there was rarely a time when he wasn't wooing me with flowers, picnics, movies, or little love notes written on dinner napkins, my heart just wasn't sure about him. He seemed too good to be true and I was waiting for it to come to an end. But he never gave up, and God had a plan.

That summer I left for my first mission trip to Venezuela and didn't see him for two weeks. I was surprised by how much I missed someone I wouldn't even call my boyfriend.

The night I returned he was on my doorstep within minutes, and we shared what would become the first of many sweet kisses.

For the next two years we were inseparable, and I would like to say the rest is history, but the story gets a little ugly before our happily-ever-after even has a chance. Jay was feeling led into ministry and was prompted to attend Indiana Wesleyan University by our Young Adult Pastor, mentor, and friend. We said a tearful good-bye with promises to call and visit as soon as we both could, but I knew (better than Jay) that it would be harder than we could imagine.

Only a few months had passed when I got the call I had been dreading. He was ending our relationship. I was blessed to have been with my two best friends and my pastor at that moment. They had to pick me up off the floor when the call ended, I was sobbing so hard. I had thought Jay was "the one" I had been waiting for all my life, and I was absolutely devastated. He had his new life in Indiana and his old one in Virginia, but he couldn't live either with his heart divided between the two.

I could do nothing to change his mind, so I picked up the broken pieces of my heart, gave them to God, and tried my best to move on. My friends from church rallied around, strengthening me. Instead of drowning in my sorrow, I regained the vitality that had been drained out of me by constantly trying to mend what couldn't be fixed. I learned to enjoy a life that didn't center around one person exclusively. It was hard, but God taught me contentment through Him alone and joy spilled over into every facet of my life.

Jay's first year away at college came to an end, and he returned home for the summer. We attended the same church, had the same friends, so we could not avoid one another for long. I would catch him looking my direction, and our eye contact made it obvious we still felt for one another.

Barely a week had gone by when he invited me over. He admitted he had made a mistake by breaking up with me, said he missed me, loved me, and wanted to start over. I agreed to give us another chance. We picked up right where we left off, but I secretly doubted his intentions. I wanted this. I wanted *him,* forever, but, understandably, I believed he would likely break up with me again when he returned to school in the fall. I needed to protect my heart so I didn't fully give it to him, although he had truly given his to me. I maintained a certain distance and refused to allow my vulnerability to be exposed. I figured we would have a great last summer together, at best.

But leaving that space allowed more than just doubt to creep in. Someone unexpected was waiting in the wings.

The summer mission trip to Russia was just around the corner and to say

I was excited is an understatement. I felt like my entire life as a Christian had led me to this point. We were holding a two-week long evangelical camp for the teenagers of Vladimir, Russia. Our single pastor (the veteran speaker of the trip) had spent a considerable amount of time helping me prepare, and we had grown close. He was not only our pastor, but one of our dearest friends as well. We both trusted and respected him implicitly.

Before we left, Jay had confided in him his love for me and his intention to propose when we returned. I didn't have a clue. Jay wanted it to be a surprise, so he hadn't even discussed marriage with me!

One night in Russia, I shared with our pastor that I didn't believe Jay was ever planning on marrying me, so I was going to end the relationship. He did not try to dissuade me. He sensed the possibility I felt something for him, so instead of allowing me to put my trust back in Jay, he purposely withheld what he knew in order to leave the door open for himself.

Jay had the most spectacular proposal planned for me. It would have been any girl's dream! All of our friends were going to hike up one mountain and Jay would lead us up another to a candlelit picnic on the rocks. When we got to the top, I would look out at the view and see our friends holding up the letters that would spell, "Marry Me."

That would never happen. The night I returned from Russia we went for a walk. As I was choking out the words of a breakup, he anticipated it and hastily pulled the ring from his pocket for a mock proposal.

Totally unprepared and in shock, I said yes and *voilà!* Two very confused people got engaged. The unraveling of my life was like a train wreck that everyone could see coming, but me. I was not ready, but he was pushing me so hard.

The following three months were full of betrayals, fights, and hurt feelings until we broke up…again.

I spent a few months sorting myself out and seeking God's will until one lonely night coming home alone from a Christmas party, my eyes were suddenly opened. I realized he was the one person on one earth that I didn't want to live without. He had relentlessly fought for me for so long; unlike anyone I'd ever known outside of God. He truly loved me. I didn't know it, but Jay had been specifically praying that God would change my heart and bring me back to him. I believe with all my heart that He did. Hopeful, I dialed his number….

On February 14th 1999, while sharing a Valentine's kiss good night, Jay gave me the one and only pear-shaped diamond ring he had saved all those months. This time there was nothing but celebrating our engagement and all that God had brought us through.

All good fairy tales tell the story of a tender young couple overcoming many obstacles before they can live happily ever after. The brilliant beauty of our love story is that true love didn't happen the way we thought it would. I am so glad that God's way was not our way. The almighty Father knew that, for us, there were lessons we both had to learn and He had allowed us to be pressed hard to learn them. Our trials engrained in us forever that true love always hopes, always trusts, always perseveres. And they have enabled us to have a joyful marriage, twelve years and counting.

HOLLY BLEVINS is a wife and mom living in the quaint little town of Berryville, Virginia. She loves spending time with her friends and family, leading worship at church, hiking, and river tubing down the Shenandoah! Her three greatest accomplishments in life are her children—Elliana, Samuel, and Evangeline Joy.

# May I Have This Dance?
## The Matt and Steph Story

* * *

### STEPHANIE KRAMM

My tiny six-year-old fingers gently brushed over the two porcelain figurines resting on top of my grandmother's dresser. A little blond-haired boy and a brown-haired girl dancing. "This is me and this is my husband!" I proudly announced to my sister.

Several years later, I served as a junior counselor at a camp my grandfather helped build in the mountains of East Tennessee. One warm summer evening, a blond-haired, blue-eyed missionary kid named Matt, also a junior counselor, kept staring at me. Uncomfortable under his gaze, I averted my eyes.

The next morning as I approached the gym for registration, Matt stood at the door staring at me again. He swung the door open, flashed a giant, boyish grin, and followed me inside. This friendly boy grew on me and before long something inside me said, *"This is the person you're going to marry—or someone exactly like him."*

Only 15 years old, I'd never felt that way about anyone before, so I decided not to make my feelings too obvious. Yet, in my journal I wrote: *He has the strongest faith in God...you can see the love of Jesus shine right through him.*

Matt and I developed a casual friendship and admired each other from a distance. Yet, when summer ended, we decided to write each other. In my journal I confided: *I didn't think a guy like that really existed or that I would actually ever meet one...* It encouraged me to wait for a man just like that to fall in love with instead of going for less than the best.

The next summer, Matt and I returned to camp. At one point we shared our feelings with each other, discovering we both felt the same way. It seemed as though we floated along with the clouds. He would serenade me with his guitar and make me melt inside when he smiled at me. I came home glowing and told my friends and family about this amazing boy and how I knew he was "the one."

At the end of the summer, he and his family flew back to Southeast Asia for two years. Half a world away, we continued to keep in touch for a year, until we realized we were headed in different directions. At that time, Matt planned on returning to the States after he finished boarding school in Thailand, while I felt called to serve the Lord overseas. Fascinated by Asia ever since I was a little girl, I felt the Lord had planted a missionary interest in my heart. So, although Matt and I admired one another, it seemed evident God was closing the door on a future together. Earlier, I'd prayed God would draw us closer to Himself before we got closer to one another. He answered my prayer in a way that felt heartbreaking at the time.

I began to think maybe the Lord brought Matt into my life simply to solidify my desire to go to Southeast Asia as a missionary and to open my eyes to the needs there. After much hesitancy, I threw away all of his letters, figuring I'd never hear from him again.

During the next few years, my interest in missions increased, but I wanted to be confident overseas work was really what God was calling me to. I decided to take my first semester off college to go on a missions' trip to Southeast Asia. I heard about a place in the Philippines where I could minister, so I started taking steps to go. But God closed the door and instead opened one in Thailand. During my trip, my passion for working with Asian children grew even more, and I fell in love with the country and its people. Later, I learned that Matt and I were in Bangkok on the same day, but never saw each other. We briefly e-mailed a couple times while I was there, and he asked for a number to call so he could come see me. I still had the same feelings for him, but thought, *I don't want it to seem like I traveled all the way around the globe to chase him!* I didn't want to manipulate circumstances that weren't part of God's plan, so I never e-mailed back.

When I arrived home I was excited about missions, but a little discontented about the prospect of being a single missionary. Throughout high school, I used to go to a quiet place in the park to think and pray. An opening in the woods led to a pathway lined with trees and bushes covered with soft orange and white flowers. At the end of the trail, a stream flowed under a small bridge. One drizzly afternoon, I walked to the bridge. With shovel in hand, I dug a hole, then placed objects that represented my heart's desire into the hole. A necklace Matt had given me. A silk Thai baby's outfit, symbolizing my dream of working with Asian children. A list of qualities I desired in a husband. Things I would save for that special someone, the last item noting: *I will save a dance for him on this bridge.* I released my dreams to the Lord for his safekeeping, not knowing how God's plan would unfold for me.

Over the next two years, other boys expressed interest in me, but I never felt the same love for them as I did for Matt. Two godly guy friends shared they had strong feelings for me and wanted to pursue serious relationships. I felt very confused, thinking maybe one of them might be the one for me and I just wasn't listening hard enough for God's voice.

In the midst of my confusion, Matt randomly wrote me. Although excitement surged through me, I remained hesitant and didn't respond to him until two weeks later. As we continued to write back and forth, I kept thinking, *We can't keep writing if he isn't the one for me. I don't want my heart to be wounded all over again.*

After agonizing with my mom and sister, they encouraged me to tell him how I felt. The idea scared me because I didn't want to come across as too forward, but I also didn't want to continue something that wasn't part of the Lord's plan. So, after much thought and prayer, I nervously sent an e-mail and decided if the feelings were not mutual, we would discontinue writing altogether.

When I didn't hear from him for three weeks, I beat myself up for telling him how I felt and assumed he was ignoring the e-mail. Then, one day, my heart leaped to find his name in my inbox. He shared that he'd been vacationing with his parents at a place with no internet access. Thankful for my honest letter, he asked me about my dreams. I had no idea what his current plans were, but told him how I felt the Lord was leading me. We were both amazed to discover that since the time we stopped writing letters four years earlier, God had been growing the exact same dream in our hearts: To work with trafficked children in Southeast Asia. He also gave us both a passion for music we wanted to share with the world. We thought we were going in completely different directions, but God had us collide right into each other on the same path. I had never met anyone with dreams so similar to mine and never expected that person to be Matt. Later, he secretly applied to my college, and we were reunited for the first time in nearly five years.

In the late fall, we walked down the pathway covered with autumn leaves to my special place for the first time together. When we arrived at the little bridge, he turned toward me, reached out his hand, and said, "May I have this dance?" He was unaware I had expressed that very desire on my buried list of things I wanted to save for my special someone. After the dance, I handed him a shovel and told him to dig at a certain spot by the bridge. When he unearthed the items, I explained how I'd buried my dreams so that God could bring them to life again, in His way and in His time. Matt shared that he'd been praying for a godly wife right before I sent him the e-mail that reconnected our lives. He said at one point, before we were reunited, he had a vision of himself dancing with a brown-haired girl that looked just like me, sharing the rest of his life with her.

In the spring, I stood alone at that same bridge looking into the quiet water, not expecting to see Matt until my birthday the next day. Something made me turn around, and I looked up to see him walking toward me with his guitar in his hands. He got down on his knees, serenaded me like he did at camp so many years earlier, and asked me to dance through the rest of my life with him.

That summer, I walked down the aisle to Matt during an outdoor wedding. Violin accompaniment played "Be Thou My Vision," our theme song. God had captured our hearts, placed His vision for oppressed children in them, and given us back to each other to serve Him together.


STEPHANIE KRAMM, along with her husband, Matt, and son, Gabriel, are preparing for missionary service in Southeast Asia. Their burden for trafficked children inspired the novel *Chosen Ones,* by Eileen Hinkle Rife (OakTara).

**www.thekrammfam.blogspot.com**

# A Journey of Love

### * * *

### BETH E. PEREZ

I squirmed in the hard wooden pew as sweat trickled down my face. Although I had been in Belize almost a week, I still imagined wringing the humidity out of the air before I could breathe it. Smiling teenage girls gathered in front of the sanctuary as Reverend Young, the local pastor, announced the youth group's special music. My attention was drawn to the young man accompanying them on his guitar. "Who is he?" I whispered to Carolyn.

"That's Ron Perez, a Peace Corps Volunteer. I'll introduce you after church," she whispered back.

I had a hard time concentrating on the rest of the service as I thought back over the chain of events that had brought me to this small Nazarene church in Central America. As a young girl growing up on a Kansas wheat farm, I had always dreamed of teaching school overseas.

While attending Oral Roberts University, I approached the Dean of Education about the possibility of doing my student teaching in a foreign country. "We've never done that before," he explained.

"Then I will be the first," I promised him.

Now four years later, I was living in Belmopan, Belize, with John and Carolyn Carr, an American couple who offered me a place to stay in exchange for helping them with their two teenage daughters and their 4,000-acre cattle ranch. My career was off to a lively start. On my first day of teaching at the elementary school, I discovered a nest of tarantulas in my desk. I slammed the drawer shut before the fuzzy inhabitants could escape. *My college professors never taught me how to handle this.*

Everyone stood for the closing hymn and my mind jolted back to the present. *Now to meet Mr. Tall, Dark, and Handsome,* I thought with nervous anticipation. I followed Carolyn outside where Ron was talking with Pastor Young.

"Ron, I'd like you to meet Beth Bentrup," Carolyn said. "She's living with us while she's doing her student teaching. "

"Glad to meet you," he said with an engaging smile. We visited for a few minutes and I learned Ron was from Jackson, Michigan and had been in Belize almost 18 months. He worked for the Belizean Ministry of Lands and Survey department and was active with the youth and the Children's Home. "I'll be happy to show you around and introduce you to the other Peace Corps Volunteers," Ron offered.

"That would be great," I thanked him. *But the person I really want to get to know is you!* Actually, I had outside help with that silent wish. The Carrs and the Youngs wanted to keep Ron and me in the country as long as possible, so they decided to try their matchmaking skills. The Carrs planned activities for us at the ranch. The Youngs invited us in the evenings for supper and suggested I give Ron a hand with the youth since the group was predominately girls. Ron welcomed the additional support. My adventuresome spirit and spontaneity complimented his sound judgment and organizational skills. We discovered we enjoyed each other's company.

We looked for every opportunity to spend time together. Ron helped me organize a field trip to John's ranch for my school children, and he came along to coordinate games and activities. We helped visiting missionaries hold revivals in neighboring villages. Ron ordered Christian movies from the US and showed "free film shows" in churches and open air meetings. I entertained the children with my ventriloquist puppets, and together we led worship music with our guitars.

When we weren't working or ministering together, we embarked on scenic adventures. We swam at the Blue Hole Natural Springs, explored St. Herman's Cave, and snorkeled at the Belize Barrier Reef. Parrots squawked noisily from the treetops, and blue morpho butterflies darted among the colorful hibiscus as we trekked down tropical trails. Our friendship quickly developed into a blossoming romance.

Five months later, Ron and I traveled with other Peace Corps volunteers to the Yucatan peninsula for Christmas vacation. One morning, we left the group and found a secluded beach at the base of Tulum's ancient Mayan ruins. Sunlight sparkled off the turquoise water as I decorated a seahorse sand sculpture with shells and seaweed.

Ron sat quietly watching me. Suddenly he broke the silence. "Will you marry me?"

I looked up, wondering if the waves and wind had played tricks on my ears. Seeing the earnest expression on his face, I jumped up, brushed the sand off, and kissed him. "Yes!" I exclaimed.

Due to the timing of Ron's Peace Corps commitment and my teaching position, we decided to set the wedding date for almost two years later on August 21, 1981, Ron's 24th birthday. Ron said he wanted to wait until he was 24 to get married. (I knew this way he would always remember our anniversary.)

Ron and our friends remained in the Yucatan a few more days, but I needed to return to Belize. After completing my student teaching in December, I had accepted a teaching position in Camalote village five miles outside of Belmopan. Elma Lewis, one of the teachers in the rural school, offered to let me live with her family while I was teaching. However, on the long bus ride home, the frigid air conditioning made me seriously ill, and I developed bronchitis.

My first week at the new school was a disaster. Four classes were held simultaneously, and the one-room school house was divided by blackboards. The idea was for each teacher to talk loud enough to hold his or her class's attention, but the louder I tried to talk, the more I coughed. The principal asked me to stay home until I was feeling better. Someone suggested I take their home cough remedy, a tablespoon of kerosene and brown sugar. I was so sick, I tried it.

This "medicine" took the bronchitis to a new level, and I ended up at the local convent. The nuns took me in and nursed me back to health. They were strict and kind and had a wonderful sense of humor. The Sisters were delighted when Ron came to visit me. They'd never had a gentleman caller come to the convent. They nicknamed him Ronamiacin, because he was better than the medicine they purchased for me at the pharmacy.

A couple weeks later, I was well enough to return to the village and my school. (This time, I was much wiser about politely refusing home remedies.)

One day, Elma and I were walking from a nearby village back to Camalote. A young Belizean man started harassing me, and she stepped in between us. With all the matronly power she could muster, Elma told him, "Dis gal done got sheself a boyfriend, and I de take care of she fu he!" The man backed away and I never saw him again. Elma and I laughed all the way home.

Ron's two-year term ended but in order to stay in Belize while I fulfilled my teaching commitment, he accepted a new assignment teaching drafting to high school students at the Belize City Nazarene High School. On the weekends, he hitchhiked 50 miles to Belmopan so we could be together.

Just as we planned, we returned to the U.S. to be married on Ron's birthday in the small Kansas church where I grew up. I wore daisies in my hair and the wedding dress my grandmother made for my mother's wedding years ago. Ron met me at the altar, and we exchanged wedding vows and a kiss. This began our journey through mountain tops and valleys, full of adventures to last a lifetime.

Through the past 30 years, we know God was with us, leading and directing our paths. Ron always points back to the miracle of how a Michigan city boy and a Kansas farm girl had to travel 2,000 miles to find each other and fall in love in a small church in the tropical jungles of Belize.

BETH E. PEREZ lives with her husband, Ron, their four sons, and the family cat in Jacksonville, Florida. They've worked with Food for the Hungry's child sponsorship program in Mexico, explored Queensland, Australia and New Zealand and traveled across the continental US in an ancient RV. And the journey goes on....

# Not a Typical Love Story

### * * *

## ALISON WINFREE PICKRELL

Ours is not a typical love story. My husband-to-be and I were on opposite sides of the country with no chance of meeting each other. God had a better idea.

I grew up in Winston-Salem, North Carolina, and got a job as a special education teacher in Statesville, which is a smaller town in a rural county near Winston. All my life I had been plagued with asthma. It interfered with my plans and my career as a teacher. Because schools are cesspools of germs, I would wind up in the hospital at least once if not twice each year during my entire teaching career.

Many of my friends and family told me to move to Arizona—that's where asthmatics go to breathe better in the desert air away from many of the plants that cause allergies. I was able to get financial aid to attend the University of Arizona in Tucson and get a Masters degree in Behavior Disorders, which was a specialty in my special-education degree.

So, with much trepidation, I resigned from my job in Iredell County and moved to the campus of the University of Arizona in Tucson. I loved Tucson. Its geography was completely different from North Carolina. In North Carolina I had been surrounded by tall trees and green foliage, but now I faced stark bare mountains and cacti instead of wildflowers. It was an alien environment, and I drank it in like a potion. And my asthma did seem to improve. I found a doctor nearby and was able to keep my medication at a minimum.

After finishing my studies at the university, which took one school year, I was so enraptured I applied for jobs with every school in and around Tucson. I moved into a small apartment complex, the Bermuda Apartments, near the campus and planned on settling there for good. Unfortunately, I was in competition with all my classmates for the few job openings in the school systems I applied to.

I made several friends at the university, all female. There were no men on the horizon, and I had resigned myself to the fact that I might remain single and focus on teaching as the primary goal in my life.

Then one day, on June 25, 1978 to be exact, a man came to paint the outside of my apartment. I went out to give him a drink of water and lingered to admire his brown, tanned skin, short shorts, and dimples in both cheeks. He asked me to go out with him for ice cream at Swenson's. Even though he was a complete stranger, I found myself agreeing, which is very unlike me. I am usually cautious and afraid to step out into unknown territory. However, I felt at ease with the man who had invited me.

I found out over ice cream that Brian Pickrell was a Vietnam vet who presently worked for a company that installed windows. He was divorced with three small sons who lived with his ex-wife. He lived in the same apartment complex I did and was, in fact, the exuberant person who had disturbed me with late-night dips in the pool outside my window.

Over the next few weeks, we were together as often as possible, including a camping trip in which he slept in the back of his truck and I slept in the tent, and a trip to a dentist when a toothache became so unbearable that Brian was nearly incapacitated.

My trust and love for him grew with every day and, at last, while we lay on the grounds of the University gazing at the sky, he proposed and I accepted. I called my parents back in North Carolina in great excitement and was surprised to find some trepidation that I was engaged to someone they hadn't met. We talked about a December wedding, and I found myself engaging in all kinds of daydreams about my wedding, how it would look, and who I would invite.

That wedding was not to be, however. As the days went by, we were so in love we had a hard time putting on the brakes and not stepping into forbidden behavior. Both of us wanted to be together so badly that we made a spontaneous and potentially crazy decision to not wait until December and instead to elope to Las Vegas, of all places.

I cannot explain how this look-before-you-leap, cautious person who had always sought her parents' advice for every other decision would agree to this plan for the most important decision of my life! My only excuse is that I was in love.

We crammed into a small car with a couple Brian knew that would serve as our best man and maid-of-honor. I don't even remember their last names. His name was Jim and hers was...? She made sure I had something old, something new, something borrowed, something blue, and even a sixpence to go in my shoe. So, prepared in that way, we drove from Tucson to Las Vegas and searched for a place to get married. We found the Candlelight Wedding Chapel sandwiched between the gambling casinos and, on July 25th, 1978—exactly one month after I had met him on a ladder outside my apartment window—we did indeed get married, much to the consternation of everyone who knew me back in North Carolina.

It could've been the worst mistake of my life. We got to know each other after marriage, which, I guess, is the pattern followed by Isaac and Rebekah, Jacob and Rachel, and all the other biblical characters we've studied. I have no doubt that God was the one who brought us together. If I hadn't had asthma, I never would've wound up in Tucson at the right time to meet Brian, who was only there because of his parents.

I didn't get a job in Arizona. Instead, I got in touch with the man who had hired me in Iredell County, and he told me to come home: they had a job for me. So back we went to North Carolina and have been here ever since.

Five months later, Brian's three sons came to live with us, making me a mother overnight. Parenting is the hardest thing I've ever attempted. I thought teaching would prepare me to be a stepmother, but only living with those three rambunctious, needy boys taught me day by day how to be a mother.

Now, 33 years later, the boys are grown with children of their own, and Brian and I are still finding out new things about each other and how perfectly we mesh. I would never recommend my road to matrimony to anyone. The only reason it worked is because God was in charge from the beginning and brought the two of us together. My asthma is still a negative part of my life, but I have come to accept it and will always appreciate the part it played in bringing me together with my beloved husband, Brian.


ALISON WINFREE PICKRELL lives in Statesville, North Carolina, where she has retired from teaching special education after 30 years. After retiring, Alison turned to a passion in her life—writing—and has published four novels: *As Eagles, Unto the Least of These, Den of Lions,* and *The Last Cordate* (all OakTara).

alisonwinfreepickrell.com

# Hurricane, a Frog,
# and True Love

\* \* \*

## DONNA COLLINS TINSLEY

I knew he was a hero from the first moment I saw him. My first glimpse of Bill was of a wet, shivering, young man needing to leave the festivities to go home and get warm and dry. My daughter and I were at a wedding, and he had jumped into a pool to save a child during the reception.

A good friend had introduced us, but it was a casual meeting, one I had immediately put out of my mind. I had other things to deal with, including the challenges of a horribly dysfunctional marriage.

Several years later we both ended up at a church on the east coast of Florida. I had been divorced for two years, and he was getting over a broken engagement. I was a single mom, who lived outside of town with my daughter, enjoying a very quiet life.

I happened to be sitting by Bill on a Sunday that church ended early because of a pending hurricane.

He leaned over and said, "Do you want me to come over and ride out the hurricane with you and your daughter?"

I barely knew him outside of the earlier meeting in Orlando years back. I had heard that he was kind, loyal, and a hard worker, but I had not spent any time alone with him.

Did I need help to get through a hurricane? I had lived in Florida most of my life and, as a single mom who had survived a marriage from hell, I had learned to cope with most things by the strength of God. But he was so sincere, and I had a couch he could sleep on so I said, "Yes."

I ran home from church to start preparing for the storm and our new friend, Bill, who was coming to protect us. I cooked fried chicken and extra coffee before he arrived.

"Regina, fill up the bathtub with water. We may need it later on," I quickly said to my daughter. That is just one of those traditions you do like when they say, "boil water" if someone is giving birth.

When Bill came over, we ate and talked as the storm worsened. When the power went off, we listened by candlelight, as he told us about his traumatic childhood. I learned that he had great faith, and in one of our conversations, he mentioned he had an extreme frog phobia. Regina and Bill played cards throughout the night. He promised to take her fishing soon, and I surmised he was probably one of the few men I could trust to do that. As a sexual abuse survivor whose first husband had abused our own daughter, I still lived with trust and control issues. Having a man in our lives was something I wasn't sure about. I knew it was wrong to have that fear, but I just wasn't able to believe I could ever trust anyone to be a father to her again.

During a lull in the storm, we stepped outside, leaving the door open. We didn't think anything about it as we were only going to be out a few minutes. Much to our dismay, as we turned to walk back in, we saw a big frog hop in the house ahead of us and go behind the couch where Bill would be sleeping.

"Get that frog out of there, or I'm leaving!" my great protector friend said.

*Oh no, I'm as terrified of frogs as he is*, I thought as I grabbed a big blanket and covered the frog up with it, hoping it would stay in the blanket as I ran to the door. Southern belle that I was, I wasn't touching a frog with my bare hands. With the frog out and the door closed, we all had a good laugh about Bill protecting *us*.

Not long afterwards on New Year's Eve, Bill took my daughter and me over to visit another single mother and her kids. As we all sat around talking, while the kids played games and listened to music, I was captivated by his strong commitment to be what God wanted him to be. It was then that I started to fall in love, but I wasn't sure what Bill had in mind. He probably just thought of me as a sister, just as I had started off thinking of him as a brother. A brother who shows up during storms or if you need your car fixed or your daughter wants to go fishing.

One day I said to Bill, "I know we both have been thinking of each other as brother and sister, but I have to be honest and tell you that, since we started praying together, I have been having some strong feelings. I think I am falling in love."

Did he grab me and kiss me? No. He said, "I'll be right back. I need to take a walk and think."

He hugged me as he left and so that made the anxiety within me lessen. The funny thing was, we had been praying together for the Lord to send the right man to be a father to my daughter and a husband for me. He had heard me crying one night, telling my mom on the phone that I would probably never get married again and had offered to pray for and with me.

Six months later, we were married. It was in July 1980.

One day right before we got married, we were visiting some friends who had just had their fifth child. He looked at me and said, "I hope nine months from the day we get married, you have a baby."

But that didn't happen.

Storms continued to plague us but not the kind that first brought us together. At age 15, my daughter started a downward spiral that was brought on by the drug addiction her biological father had introduced her to. I found that Bill was committed to parenting a daughter that many men would have given up on. Many times he went with me to look for her on the streets of Daytona.

"Why would she run away?" he said once. "Doesn't she realize I love her as if she were my own child?"

Holding each other, we waited for the next storm together. There was a lull when a judge sent her home to our custody because she was pregnant. She had a baby girl the day she turned 18.

We were still praying to have a baby of our own. It had been five long years. When Regina left home six weeks later, taking our first grandchild with her, I thought Bill's heart would break in two. That only enhanced the stress I felt each month when I would hope I was pregnant and then realize I wasn't.

"I know we are going to have the opportunity to parent, maybe even children that really need someone like I did as a boy," he said as he put his arms around me. Bill and his siblings had been separated at one point in their childhood because of an abusive father.

Not long afterward, Regina got married and during that period I finally conceived. We had two beautiful daughters—Amber and then, later on, Shiloh. It looked like the *good life* that Bill always wanted for his family might become a reality. But after a few years, Regina and her husband divorced, and my daughter went back to her former lifestyle.

At one point it nearly was too much for even my *protector* to bear when several more children were born to my daughter in the midst of arrests. We were trying to take care of two grandchildren and our own little girls. Work was slow, and depression became his daily friend; we both nearly went under. But one day Bill decided he was sick of the depression, doctors, and medications.

"I had taken my eyes off of God," he told me.

He decided then and there to do the business of making things right through prayer. When he got off his knees that day, he chose a different way to live, one that cleared the path through the storms.

Thirty-one years later, I am grateful that, although life has been very chaotic, I have always had Bill's love.

I may still have to save him from frogs, but in Bill's love I have seen an example of a husband for all the storms of life.


DONNA COLLINS TINSLEY, wife, mother, and grandmother, lives in Port Orange, Florida and has been included in several book compilations. She is a lover of the Lord Jesus and a sister among you.

Find her at Facebook, Somebody's Mother Online Prayer-Support Group, **http://thornrose7.blogspot.com/** or email her at **thornrose7@aol.com.**

# Still...

## * * *

## JENNY JOHNSON

I f we were starting out today, I might be called a cougar. Back then, I was just the older woman his mother warned him about. We grew up in the same small Southern town, but not together. A few years in age difference can be a generation apart when you're young. I was almost five when he was born. I was 15—old enough to be his baby-sitter—when he was 10. He was a freshman at the local high school the year I entered college several states away.

By the time we noticed each other, he was just starting college and working part-time at a grocery store. I was finishing college and starting life over as a working girl who had discovered a whole new world away from the dot on the map where we grew up.

In our hometown there was a little mom and pop grocery store—now long gone—that delivered to your door and charged to your account. He worked there from the time he was 16 through high school and until after he finished college. I shopped there for the family groceries. The setting would never appear on a list of The 10 (or 10,000) Most Romantic Places to Meet. It was a cement block box with concrete floors and a limited selection of goods. It was also God's incubator for real and lasting love.

At the beginning, we only eyed each other with interest from across the grocery aisles. There was no conversation, no clandestine meeting at the candy display or near the vegetable bins...but there was chemistry. I wondered who that tall and handsome young man was who looked so sweet. He wondered if the girl with the black hair was available. But no words were exchanged. This was 1972, after all. Fine Southern ladies had their standards.

I did my homework...my background checker was my mother's friend who said he was engaged. "Oh, honey," she was a talker and knew everybody, "those two are *thing and thing*." And she intertwined her fingers to show how close they were.

Really?

I saw his "friend" showing off his class ring, which she wore around her neck, one day at his grocery store. It didn't dampen my interest, and she didn't know her competition. Besides, I had a secret weapon. I had Daddy.

My dear (now departed) daddy was an "arranger" of the first order. It wasn't the first time he tried, rest his soul. My younger sister had been wed for years, and I suppose he thought I was nearing spinsterhood. Legend has it that Daddy "put in a good word for me" with the young man at the grocery store, as if I needed taking care of. I was a grown woman with a life of my own, for heaven's sake.

It must have been a *really good word*, because the next thing I knew, I was—yes—in the grocery store, when I heard…

"Would you like to go…?"

And I said, "Why, yes I would, thank you."

I wore a borrowed dress with purple and pink tulips on it. The date was perfection. He was such a gentleman, and by the end of the evening, I was…to use the expression of the day…"snowed."

He didn't call. I waited, not patiently, but in vain. He *never* called.

What happened? I was *so sure*. What went wrong? What did I say? What did I not say?

I really didn't know. *He just did not call.*

I didn't give up easily—any excuse to go to that grocery store—even if we didn't need anything but dog food. I bought a lot of dog food that summer. *Still nothing.*

A year passed, maybe more. I kept going, hoping to see him, whenever I was home from wherever I'd moved. Hope springs eternal. One day, I was shopping for…whatever…when I overheard a couple talking about their son who was really sick. I'd never seen them before…but I knew who they were.

Their son soon received a special get-well package in the mail filled with all the goodies I knew he would like…and that would help him remember…*me*.

It worked. Gradually, slowly.

"Are you willing…?"

"Yes, I'd be glad to."

"Can you come over and help out with…?"

"Of course. I'll bring a friend."

"Would you like to go with me to…?"

"I would. Yes, that would be nice."

We took up right where we'd left off, a year and a half before. I listened to his reason for not calling…something to do with waiting until he took care of business and broke an engagement and not involving me…very noble. I believed him.

My ego was glad to have him back, but now there was another problem. Time had passed…water was under the bridge…and I was no longer crazy infatuated. After all, suppose I changed my mind? The world was big, and the possibilities were endless. What if someone else came along I liked better? He seemed to understand.

"Okay, so we'll keep it light."

"Yes, good idea. We'll 'sing in the sunshine'…not worry too much about what happens next."

That worked for a while.

But then there came a day when I had to choose. Did I risk the keeper bird in front of me for two lesser ones that might be waiting in the bush? This man, for all of his youth, was not one for me to lose. All of my eggs went into his basket. I couldn't take a chance, regardless of the cost to my jealously guarded freedom.

And then he made me wait. Great strategy.

My clock was ticking, and I had him by almost five years. I fidgeted. I squirmed. I hinted. Finally, at long last…

"Will you…?"

"Hmmm, let me think…Yes, I will!"

We had a home wedding and honeymooned at Myrtle Beach. I thought I'd died and gone to heaven. Fairy tales, sometimes, are real.

We had a tiny upstairs apartment and the smallest, oldest imaginable black and white TV.

He worked three jobs, and I worked on my doctorate. I found out how funny he was…such a great trait in a man. I worried that I'd robbed him of his younger years. I said I'd get a facelift when the time came. We were opposites on nearly everything. He found out I really did know how to argue. I found out he'd meant it when he told me, "I can't solve all of your problems."

We wanted children but not now…later. We needed more time for just the two of us. We had four years before God intervened and sent us two little babies in one year. He was as good a mother as I was and a better father. He often had to do both jobs after working all day while I taught late classes and came dragging home at 9 or 10 at night.

We played and loved and lived through heart surgeries and hysterectomies, missing pets and lost loved ones. Sometimes we liked each other less than others, but loved each other more all the time. As I write this, it's been 37 years—nearly a generation, two careers, two children, three grandchildren--and the usual things that wear us down and pull us apart. I should be tired of him. He *surely* should be tired of me. We should have "outgrown" each other by now. By the odds, as a couple we could be old news with both of us working on number two, or three, or four. What a wonderful gift to find I *still* want to be with him more that with anyone on earth, *still* need to be with him, *still* dread to spend even one night away from him even after all these years.

To quote an old and overused phrase, I do believe it was "a marriage made in Heaven." I believe that a creative and loving God with a sense of humor (and a little help from Daddy), out of all the possible combinations available, without any help from an Internet profile, and as unlikely a match as we were, chose us to spend a lifetime together.

I'm *still* working on a way to stay married in Heaven and make it an eternity together.

> "Therefore what God has joined together, let no one separate."
> MARK 10:9, NIV

JENNY JOHNSON has worked and written for years as a university professor in Special Education. Now retired and working part-time, an item on her "never-too-late list" is fiction writing. Her first romantic suspense novel, *The Taxi*, was published in 2012 (OakTara).

http://jennywjohnson.blogspot.com/
http://www.jennyjohnsonauthor.com

# Forever In Your Eyes
## A Love Letter to Molly

\* \* \*

## JOHN A. MIZERAK

Dear Molly,

There are so many things I want to say to you that it's hard to know where to begin, so I'll just start at the beginning of *us*.

We met in October of 1980 and I remember you told me you "saw forever in my eyes"; that strong soul-connection frightened you. I have to admit I saw a radiant smile and long legs! I'm sorry I was so shallow, but you learned to love me anyway. Even though we spent four years getting to know one another and got married in 1984, I believe our true love affair began the day you received Jesus Christ in 1995. At the time, not understanding your new faith, I thought you were crazy. I thought intimacy in our marriage was going to suffer. But two years later, God grabbed my heart as well.

The first 10 years were a challenge because of our polar opposite personalities. You were strong-willed, and I was laid-back. At the time, I wasn't sure why God ever put us together. We were close to divorce, and it felt like there was complete ruin in our family of five until God stepped in. We worked hard at making a great marriage and family from that point on, but I have to admit, you worked harder than I did. From the time Christ entered your life, you became more and more selfless. You wanted to serve God and me, and set a biblical example for our family. If I have one regret, it's that I did not fully engage you to understand your heart in those early years. I know at the time you didn't feel appreciated or loved, but that certainly wasn't the case. I loved you so much and I still do, but I couldn't always express it!

Though things got better as we grew together as a family in Christ, we still had a long way to go. I'm sure you remember that pivotal night in 2005, when one of the kids was about to ask me a question at the dinner table. Realizing that Dad wouldn't know the answer, they turned to you. I didn't notice, but I remember you were deeply impacted and asked me to forgive you for creating an environment of disrespect. From that point on you encouraged me to become the spiritual leader of our home. Because of that freedom, I not only became a better leader, I became a better husband, father, and even businessman.

Our marriage blossomed from that time forward. You chose to become more submissive and encouraged me to continue to lead even though it was totally against your personality to do so. I felt so loved as you trusted God to work in my heart. It amazes me that, when someone is truly humbled, how it can dramatically and positively change the lives of the people around them. I am now a living example of how that principle can play out. I was so excited to see that, after 26 years, we finally got our marriage in order, and we were ready to soar into the next half of our life together. We had made grand plans about having our children early and being young enough to enjoy the second half of our marriage after they were grown. That's the funny thing about building your life around your own plans; God may have different ones.

I have to admit, when you started to have difficulty speaking, I was mildly amused. After listening to you talk on and on for so many years, I didn't know how to act when I had to do all the talking. I simply thought you were having a chemical imbalance from menopause or something similar to the depression and panic attacks that led you to the Lord in 1995. I remember when we went to the doctor on February 21, and we were forced to have an MRI on your brain. I was thinking two things: *Gee, I'm hungry, I wonder what are we having for dinner,* and, *How are we going to pay for psychiatric help?*

It's amazing how quickly your thinking and life can change. I was wondering why the radiation technician got serious and asked me to go talk to the radiologist. I wasn't prepared for what I was about to see. My life was turned upside down as I looked at an image of your brain with a mass the size of my fist in it. As you can imagine, I was shocked. The doctor told me to keep myself together, for your sake, and immediately get you to the hospital in Fairfax. I was numb. I knew I had to tell you what was happening, and I'm sorry that I wasn't gracious when I blurted it out. Thank you for not panicking. The strength you displayed that day and through this entire ordeal was so comforting, it made us all stronger. I know the peace you displayed came from your deep trust in God.

Everyone was amazed at how quickly you recovered from brain surgery. I was so proud of you when, after only one week, we were home, exercising at the gym, and going for walks. I was sure that everything was going to be fine, and we would witness a complete healing on this side of eternity.

As the days went on, and you began to improve slightly, I was so excited to get back to normal. It seemed like everything was on track. That was, until that day early in April when we went to get the next MRI. I was sure it was going to show an improvement. Instead, we received the devastating news that the tumor had not only returned but had grown bigger in a mere six-week period than it had before it was taken out. Again, I was amazed at your faith. As the entire family cried, you decided to fully surrender to God and comforted us without shedding a tear. Even though our relationship had started over 30 years prior to that day and your love for me began to flourish in 1995, for the first time in my life, I fully learned what love was all about.

As you spent the next two months in a slow physical decline, I was blessed to become your full-time nurse. It was very frustrating knowing that we were on an island, isolated from the medical community, because we chose not to have the standard treatment of chemo and radiation. I was honored to become your primary caregiver.

One never knows how they might handle this type of adversity until they go through it. I never knew I could care for you the way I did. If you had asked me just six months before if you thought I could handle what I was forced to do, I would have said, "NO WAY!"

I remember how, early in our relationship, you wouldn't let me sit in the adjacent room when you had to go to the bathroom because you were afraid I would hear. But now you allowed me to care for your every need and actually laughed about how poorly I did it at times. Wow, honey, we really grew over the years.

The saddest day of my life was June 1, 2011, when you went home to be with our Lord.

You were still beautiful, not having aged a bit in 30 years. Even though this time of sickness usually ravages so many of its victims, you lost only 10 pounds and still looked amazing to me.

I spent the next couple of days in a fog and forced myself to go to our church the following Sunday. Pastor had informed me that he wanted to do a tribute to you that day. He didn't want the church service to become a funeral, so he did a short five-minute tribute at the beginning of the service. It was the first of many times I turned into an emotional train wreck. I was a mess!

Afterward, there was an awkward three-minute break, and we began our normal set of upbeat praise music. I thought there was no way that I could worship God in the state of mind I found myself in. I closed my eyes and saw a picture of a triangle. God was clearly showing me that my heart was connected to His, and YOUR heart was still connected to mine.

I can't explain it, Molly, but the feeling was amazing. I felt as if your heart was transplanted into my chest. When I opened my eyes, I was worshipping God like I never had before. Contrary to my conservative nature, I was actually being demonstrative. I felt like I was floating and could have worshiped for hours.

At that exact minute, I knew everything would be all right. I knew that as I moved on with my life and pursued God's heart, I would also know your heart more and more. Our love triangle will continue at a much deeper level because of the legacy you left behind. Molly, this is the end of our earthly relationship, but it is the beginning of my deepest spiritual love affair. Thank you for your sacrifice. I now see forever in YOUR eyes! I love you!


JOHN A. MIZERAK owns a marketing business in the Washington, DC Metro area. John graduated from SUNY Buffalo in 1984 with a BA in communication. John is a widower with a family of three adult children—Chris, Samantha, Jamie—living in Purcellville, Virginia.

www.MamaMiz.com

# Matters of the Heart

### * * *

## MILLICENT NJUE

When I enrolled in college that year, I did not know that I was about to get more than I bargained for. For it was there that I met the love of my life.

It was a new beginning. I had looked forward to starting down my career path by going to college. It was the first month there, and I knew just a few people in my class. The place had so many students that I was in no hurry to get close to anyone yet. But there are no plans in matters of the heart.

A lean, good-looking young man walked up to me with his hands stretched out. He had the softest hands a man could have. And a warm grasp as well. Little did I know that, at that moment I was about to give my heart away forever. We had just begun our journey of love.

We met every day for lunch and got to know each other well. I looked forward to each new day, knowing he was going to be in it. It is the best feeling ever.

One day, he was invited for an evening party at some company he'd worked for. He asked me to accompany him there. It was a magical evening. Since we were the youngest couple, we were asked to open the dance. He chose our favorite love song. And when we took to the floor, it might just have been the two of us. No one else mattered when he gazed into my eyes.

In no time, I was in deep. Love had finally come to dock. We took endless coffee for an opportunity to sit across and stare shyly into each others' eyes. We spoke about everything too. But when it came to emotional matters, we did not need to speak much. He understood my feelings and I, his. Words were not always necessary. His love was in the way he smiled. And in his touch. He had a nice laugh too.

We went to the movies every Saturday. It was our sacred routine. It felt so nice cuddling up to him in the dark, well aware that it was a public place. And boy, could he kiss. Everything he did was an art.

We took walks in the park. There is nothing like a touch of nature in the arms of the one you love. I felt so secure because he towered over me. We shared so many stories of our growing up. We connected so well. I loved this man, in a way I could love no other.

I discovered myself in the arms of the one I loved. He awakened feelings that I was not aware of in me. I found myself longing to be with him all the time. He fit into my life like a jigsaw puzzle piece. Though he did not speak much, our bond was strong.

In life, you only meet one such person. The one who completes you and fills you with so much feeling. The one whose touch brings goose bumps all over. The one in whose arms you get a touch of heaven because nothing else compares to a moment in his embrace. The one who understands your needs, even though unspoken. The one with whom you connect in such a magical way it seems almost divine.

We did all the crazy things lovers the world over do. We kissed in the rain and visited so many places. We held hands and spoke on the phone all night. It was the natural thing to do when the person on the other end seemed to be holding the keys to my life. Sometimes we forgot about those around us and disappeared to our own little world. Just like that, we could lock out all else and sink into our own little paradise.

Many times we would sit in a coffee shop until closing time and had to be asked to leave. It felt right sitting across from him, searching his eyes and seeing my feelings mirrored in his eyes. It felt even better when we clasped our hands together and said sweet nothings across the table. I loved watching him looking so vulnerable to the wills of love.

Everything about him was so special. The touch of his hand was electric. It seemed natural for me to love him with all my heart. The days we were apart were unbearable because all I could think of was him. It was his face I saw when I fell asleep at night and him I would woke up thinking of.

As time went on, our love grew. To a point where, if all was not well with one of us, the other would know. It became increasingly hard for us to stay apart. Together is where we were meant to be. I remember those days well. Our love continued long after graduation. He went on to work with a leading research company. As I went to work elsewhere. But even then he was constantly in my mind.

We continued seeing each other, although our jobs took most of our time. Many are the times we'd leave work and spend time together at some restaurant until late. It was a struggle having the same amount of time together that we were used to at college. But somehow we made time to be together.

There is so much I loved about him. The way he stammered when overcome with emotion. Or the way he seemed unable to make up his mind when it was time to leave. He was the gentlest person I ever met. The way he smiled melted my heart.

Something special happened to me. I understood what it meant to love someone so much and allow them to follow their heart. All the wild love songs suddenly made sense to me. All the beauty of having found love and being loved back, and the power of two hearts meeting and never being apart again. The energy it takes for two lovers to make their time together memorable.

It will remain with me forever, this love. The feelings are still as fresh as if we met yesterday. There is nothing as good as finding real love and having met someone who will forever remain etched in your heart. No matter the distance, love remains. And true love never dies. Lovers might be separated, but their souls remain knit together by what they shared. Because when love is true and just, no distance can separate two people in love.

I am happy to have been loved with a love never-ending. To have found the one that holds the keys to my heart forever. I thank God for bringing us together. For the chance to have loved and truly been loved by a very special man in my life.


MILLICENT NJUE has been writing Christian articles for a long time now and delights in bringing out life's emotions through words. She lives in the city of Nairobi in Kenya. Besides her regular job she enjoys time with her husband and her three kids. Millicent has green fingers too and enjoys time at the farm in the countryside.

http://wwwunmeasuredgrace.blogspot.com/

# The List

* * *

## TARA R. ALEMANY

Over 10 years ago, a friend of mine and I were talking about relationships. My friend, Nigel, had found "The One" and was preparing to marry her. I was wrestling with the bad choices I'd made in the past and the dysfunctional model of love I'd had growing up.

I asked my friend how I would know the right person when I found him. Nigel recommended that I spend some time in prayer and reflection, and then write a list of those qualities that God would have included in the man He created especially for me. Knowing myself and that God desired a happy, Christ-centered relationship for me, what were the qualities my significant other would need to be my ideal mate?

The following list contains the qualities I came up with based on my circumstances, past experiences, desires, and needs.

- A man of strong Christian faith.
- Someone who valued honor and integrity.
- A man who would do what is right, even when it's hard.
- Someone who understood what it meant to protect his family, and who was willing to lay down his life for them.
- A man who would share the daily chores and challenges with me.
- Someone caring and compassionate.
- A man with the intellectual capacity to challenge me.
- Someone who understood and embraced the fact that I was a package deal.
- A man who could communicate his thoughts and feelings.
- Someone with whom I could disagree and even argue with, yet still feel safe, loved, and secure.

This list has saved me a lot of heartache over the years. As I met new people, I could assess them against these qualities. I hate to admit that in the intervening years, I'd only met a few single men who demonstrated more than a handful of them. Yet each quality was important to me, so I never let those relationships develop beyond friendships.

Then, in July 2011, an unexpected series of events, initiated by an errant e-mail, brought someone new into my life. Frank had been alone 10 years, while I'd been alone 12. Although he'd never formally written down his list, he knew exactly what he was looking for: his last relationship. As he put it, he wasn't looking for that woman he could live with; he was looking for the one he couldn't live without.

Within the first three weeks of our meeting, he demonstrated every single quality I'd been searching for in a man. Thankfully, in that same three-week period, he realized he couldn't live without me.

The next few months were spent deepening our relationship, making plans to meet in person (we lived 1,200 miles apart), praying and seeking God's will for our life, and anticipating a long and happy future together.

Frank began to help me in my business, and we found it fun to create things together. We often spent 12 or more hours a day together on the phone, working, playing, studying the Bible, and praying together.

During our prayers, he always thanked God for bringing me into his life, for sending him a wife he could be proud of, grow old with, and love always. While we hadn't married yet in the eyes of man, before God we each knew we belonged with the other. He loved me as his wife, and I cherished him as my husband; both of us were just waiting for that time when we could make our vows official.

When my son required school supplies, clothes, and a bit of summer tutoring, Frank sent the funds for "our son" to have what he needed. While it was hard for me to accept his gift, I knew it was exactly the response I wanted in someone I was going to spend my life with.

When my daughter, who is a dancer, injured her ankle in class one night, Frank walked me through everything I needed to know to get the best medical care for her. He was pleased that his decades of experience as a First Aid and CPR instructor for the American Red Cross could be put to good use.

Although he'd never had children of his own, Frank looked forward to being a stepfather to my children, and being whatever father figure they needed him to be. He'd even asked if it was okay with me if he adopted them someday. His love for me extended to my children. He wanted nothing more than to create a family out of the two of us, my two kids and our cat, and his two dogs.

As a former Auxiliary State Police officer, he was passionate about guns and gun safety and was thrilled to hear that my son was hoping to attend a gun safety training course at our local shooting range when he turned 12 in March. While this was not *my* idea of a fun thing to do, Frank understood my son in ways that a mother never could.

He volunteered to take my son to the range and insisted that I come too. He emphasized that it was important I knew and learned the same things about guns that my son did so I could reinforce the rules at home. As resistant as I was to the whole idea, Frank wore me down and looked forward to being able to share this experience with us.

Unfortunately, this was one of many experiences we never got to share together. As much as we joked about whose "kids" were going to be more trouble when we blended our families (my two-legged or his four-legged), Frank never got to partake of that event. As swiftly as he swept into my world and turned everything upside-down, Frank was gone, felled unexpectedly by an enlarged heart. I was left to carry on alone, finishing the things we set out to do together.

The book that I was writing when we met will soon be published. He was my first reader for everything I wrote, and I miss hearing his thoughts and impressions.

Next month, I'll attend the black belt test that I've spent the last four years studying and practicing for, and that Frank had planned to attend with me. He was so very proud of me for all that I had accomplished, and wanted to celebrate with me when that milestone was achieved.

In two more weeks, I'll take my son to the shooting range, and we'll attend the gun safety class together. It's still not my idea of a fun thing to do, but Frank convinced me it was the *right* thing to do for my son.

After his death, I adopted Frank's "kids" and blended our families, just as we'd planned to do together. Although it hasn't been an easy transition for them or for us (they were well-loved, but not well-disciplined), they have truly become special members of our family.

Life will never be the same. Yet I've had the blessing of finding the man that God had made for me. And I've had the honor of fulfilling Frank's dearest wish: to find that woman he just couldn't live without. I still have a note he wrote that told me just that.

While I have been forever changed by the love we shared, we didn't have nearly enough time together. When Christmas came and he wasn't here, fresh questions appeared. What was his favorite Christmas carol? He loved music so much that none of his friends or family could tell me. Did he like colored lights or white ones on the tree? Simple questions like these continue to pop up every day.

I had looked forward to a lifetime of finding out answers to my questions and unlocking the mystery that is another person. Instead, I raise our family and look forward to the day when I can see his face and hear his laugh once more. I plan to give him an earful when I do!

What will be the blink of an eye for him until we're together again will be a lifetime for me. Yet I'm thankful for the faith that we shared and the sure and certain knowledge that, while our future together here on Earth was cut short, our future together in Heaven will last an eternity.

That was the greatest blessing of my list. My years alone taught me to love myself. Waiting for God's best for me taught me patience. Committing to wait upon God's timing saved me pain and heartache, as well as saving me from settling for something less than God had planned.

And living a life within God's will for me? Well, that was just priceless.

TARA R. ALEMANY is a speaker, writer, and social media consultant. Her other titles include an ebook, *The Plan that Launched a Thousand Books*, and a coauthored book, *The Character-Based Leader*. She lives with her two children in Sherman, Connecticut.

Connect with her online at **http://alewebsocial.com.**

# Broken Hearts, Redeemed

## * * *

## ANDREA ARTHUR OWAN

To say I was unlucky at love my first three years of college is an understatement. My college campus was littered with jagged fragments of my heart; pieces carved up and cast aside by smooth-talking boys. Insecure, craving love and attention, I naïvely believed they really cared for me and kept their "promises."

By my sixth semester, I wised up. It helped that God brandished my self-destructive behavior before me like a glaring neon sign. No longer would I surrender my heart for manipulation and ravaging. Instead, I'd guard it ferociously.

I'd date on *my* terms. No more attachments. If necessary, I'd hurt before getting hurt. Never would I fully trust anyone again.

Then I met Chris. He entered the school and my life in the summer of '79—a scared freshman arriving early to attend preseason soccer practices and find a job. His cheery, innocent face divulged naïveté. A friend of mine introduced us. I smiled warmly, shook Chris's sweaty hand, and welcomed him to school. Then I forgot about him.

Several weeks later, Chris wandered into the athletic training room where I worked as an intern and asked me to tape his stress-fractured foot because his team trainer was away. So I obliged him, then sent him to practice, but not before a thought raced through his mind while I deftly applied adhesive tape to his foot. *This woman is going to be the mother of my children.*

Thankfully Chris waited two years to divulge that internal revelation. But thereafter, he arrived daily in the training room to hand me his tape rolls and stick his foot on the table in front of me. According to him, I provided the best taping he'd ever received. "I can actually run and kick without pain," he'd gush. He seemed nice, and he *was* cute, but no sparks flew when he entered my personal space. I just did my job.

But as providence had it, my sorority interacted a lot with his fraternity.

So one afternoon, on a beautiful fall day, my friend Carol and I entered his fraternity to visit. Chris was busy mounting a bulletin board—a freshman pledge project—to an entryway wall and excitedly waved us over to appreciate his handiwork. Afterwards, on the way up the stairs, Carol and I sneaked an unnoticed look at him. Being a sports medicine major, his well-developed thighs and posterior physique grabbed my attention.

"Nice legs," I whispered to Carol.

"Yeah." She nodded energetically and laughed.

"Ah, he wouldn't be interested in us anyway. We're too old for him." I shrugged.

Carol concurred with another laugh, and we ascended the stairs without another backward glance, comment, or thought. Acquaintance status was as far as we got that first year.

During the summer of 1980, I took more notice of him. In fact, I did more than notice. The night I realized—with a jolt—that I was attracted to him, I retreated. *Quickly.* I knew my good friend Sarah* liked him, and I refused to do something ruinous—to all of us.

Yet a month later, after school resumed in the fall of 1980, when I answered my ringing phone, Chris's voice greeted me.

"Are you going to be at the house tonight working on the float?" he asked. Our sorority and his fraternity were doing homecoming together, and we planned a night of stuffing chicken wire holes with little squares of colorful tissue paper.

"Yes, but only for a short while."

"Okay, I work until nine. *Promise* you won't leave until I talk to you?"

"Okay…I promise."

"Good. Thanks! Bye."

I hung up the phone and stared at it for several seconds. *What brought that on?* I wondered. *He sounds so urgent; kind of distressed.*

That night, while I was squeezed between the dining room wall and an expansive section of chicken wire, Chris bolted through the doorway and stopped. Once he located me, he sprinted across the floor and squatted down to peer behind the float section.

"Do you have a date for homecoming?" he asked breathlessly. No "hi" or small talk. Just the blurted-out question.

"No," I responded hesitantly. *Do I really want to go?*

*name changed

"Well, will you go with me to homecoming?" Chris raced through the question so quickly I knew it took every ounce of his courage to utter it.

"You want *me* to go with *you?*" I squinted at him. His cornflower blue eyes begged for my response. "What about Sarah?" I demanded. "Aren't you going with *her?*"

Chris sat back on the floor, stunned. "Why would I ask Sarah?"

"Aren't you *dating* her?" *I sound like an inquisitor.*

"No!" Chris cried vehemently. His countenance and demeanor revealed his genuine shock and confusion.

*Oh, God*, I thought, *I know this scenario all too well. He's clueless. He doesn't know women's hearts at all, and he's about to shatter hers.*

I laid the tissue paper down, locked eyes with his, and sighed. "Well*, she* thinks you are, and she's expecting to go with you. If you want me to be your date, we're going to take care of this right now. I'm not going to lose Sarah as a friend."

"Okay," Chris squeaked and searched for Sarah, who worked on a different float section on the other side of the room. Several other friends were asked to join us.

Six of us settled at a table and painfully uncovered intentions, misunderstandings, and heartbreak. Tempers flared. Tears poured. Genuine apologies were offered, and love and forgiveness ruled. Friendships remained intact, though wounds required months of healing.

Chris and I started our courtship. For hours we'd sit on his fraternity's living room couch, in front of a fire, talking about dreams and life. Mostly he relived his success as a high school soccer and football player, and I dutifully "Ooh'ed and ahh'd."

Chris faithfully escorted me home each night to my sorority house door, and told me what a nice evening he'd had, before saying good night. During those awkward moments, we'd engage in pointless small talk as Chris shifted back and forth on his feet.

On one of those nights, I had a mental conversation with myself while we walked. *I'll make this easy for him. I'll open the door, turn around, and quickly say good night.*

As we approached the house, I promptly located my keys and unlocked the door. As I turned to say good night, Chris planted a speedy kiss on my lips, then bolted down the sidewalk. No warning, no good-bye. I stood on my front porch, laughing, as I watched him sprint down the sidewalk to his house. Our memorable first kiss. *That must have taken all of his courage too!*

Several months later, while we peered through a car dealership window, on a cold Midwest night, he divulged to me that he loved me.

And this time it was different. Chris had cracked my veneer. We had so much in common, so much to talk about. (He came with a damaged heart too, care of his family.) With him, I could be myself. With him, I felt safe. With him, I was willing to be vulnerable. And I was rewarded.

Chris's ultimate proposal wasn't too romantic. Four weeks after I left for graduate school, he awakened me with a 2:00 a.m. phone call to blurt out another question. "Will you marry me?" he asked, voice quavering.

Despite the unusual setting and time, I said yes and told him to call my dad for permission. He did.

In August, 1983, we were married, and I worked while he finished his last year of engineering school. We then headed to California where, six years later, I became the mother of his children.

I thought I could counteract hurt by living a life full of superficial, disconnected relationships. That, at least, seemed safer. But God, in his infinite wisdom and tender mercy knew better and planned accordingly.

For nearly 29 years, the Supreme Author of Love has patiently worked to replace our broken, hardened hearts with new models—ones fashioned to receive true love, and fully give it in return, even if it sometimes hurts. Together Chris and I have ascended spiritual mountaintops and crawled through spiritual valleys. We've nursed each other through grave illnesses and waited endless, stressful hours for one another in recovery rooms. Successfully raising two beautiful sons infuses us with joy, but our daughter's death left our hearts hemorrhaging and nearly destroyed. We've battled the world, each other, and ourselves.

And God has shepherded us through every inch of life, teaching us early that "divorce" would be banned from our vocabulary, a record of wrongs is not to be kept, and the sun mustn't set on our anger. He has taught us just how fragile—and priceless—we are, to him and to one another.

Our story lives; daily our love grows deeper.

By his grace and mercy alone, we are broken hearts, redeemed.


ANDREA ARTHUR OWAN is a writer, speaker, and educator. Her work has appeared in a variety of publications. She currently resides in Arizona with her beloved and their youngest son. Born in California and raised in Hawaii, Andrea dreams of dividing her writing, romancing, and ukulele-playing time between these two places.

**http://brokenheartsredeemed.blogspot.com**

# Annie's Impossible Love
## My Parents' Love Story

\* \* \*

### ANNE MCKAY GARRIS

S tanding stock-still, offering plate in hand, John James McKay finally realized he was staring at the charming young lady sitting in the front pew beside her distinguished-looking parents. He turned quickly away, but not before the young lady's mother raked him with a look that clearly said, "Who are you? Why are you staring at my daughter?"

John had enjoyed a brief conversation with Annie Anderson at a young people's meeting. Since then he thought of her constantly, reminding himself that she was not for him. Her father was Judge Clifford Anderson. He had been a respected Congressman in the Confederacy, and Annie's family lived in a neighborhood of elegant homes bordered by a charming park.

John's family lived in a row house, far from the socially prominent Andersons.

John's father was not even employed. Sent from England, to manage a plantation in Georgia, he had struggled so unsuccessfully that he finally retired to his religious studies, leaving his six sons to support the family.

Although courting Annie was clearly out of the question, John frequently sat beside her in Sunday school class, enjoying her company. To his delight, she welcomed him, asking unexceptionable questions about the lesson. He soon knew his heart was lost forever.

One Sunday after church he approached Annie and her parents. "I wonder, Miss Anderson, if I might be allowed to escort you home from church today," he asked.

Annie greeted him cordially.

"This is Mr. John McKay," she told her parents. "We met at the Young People's meeting. May I accept his invitation?"

Judge Anderson glanced at the young man, then at his wife. Seeing the speculative gleam common to any mother of a marriageable-age daughter, he smiled and offered John his hand. "Make sure she behaves," he joked, knowing

Annie's behavior was always faultless.

Mrs. Anderson, believing her husband would not have welcomed the young man had he known a shadow of doubt about him, added, "And perhaps, having gotten her safely home, you would do us the honor of joining us for Sunday dinner."

"The honor is mine," answered John, with impeccable manners, not believing his good fortune.

Annie's mother smiled to see her daughter practically skipping to keep up with her long-legged escort. He leaned down and said something that made Annie laugh as he tucked her hand onto his arm. They proceeded at a much slower pace, her face upturned to his with a look that caused her mother to murmur to her husband, "Tell me about this young man."

"Why, my dear, I was going to ask you to tell me. I know nothing about him. The only McKay I've ever known was a lay minister who got himself into trouble with the Presbyterian church and asked me to represent him—something about breaking church rules by traveling on Sunday. He lives in South Georgia. Good man! Very devout!" Judge Anderson gazed earnestly at the flower gardens along the way, hoping to conceal his amusement.

"Clifford, that will not do. You must find out more. I have never encountered a Mrs. McKay in Macon. Do you suppose he even has a mother?"

"Most people do," replied her incorrigible husband.

"Now stop that," she demanded. "Promise you will find out who his family is without delay."

"Yes, dear," he said.

Sunday dinner went well. John McKay turned out to be exceptionally pleasant company. His compliments to Mrs. Anderson were thoughtfully expressed. He adored Annie with his eyes while chuckling at her brother's jokes and conversing intelligently with her father. Annie remained quiet and demure in an unaccustomed way.

*Not bad!* thought the Judge and quickly made it his business to learn all he could about his daughter's new friend. Annie became a creature of joy and delight, suffering her brother with patience, treating her parents with unusual affection. She never mentioned John, but her eyes sparkled when someone else did. Seeing this, Judge Anderson was enormously reluctant to confide in his wife what he had discovered.

John and Annie's encounters were carefully contained within the confines of church events and the entertainments hosted at Annie's home or the homes of her friends. Mrs. Anderson seemed content with this until one day she rushed, uninvited, into her husband's study.

"Clifford," she said, standing stiffly before him, refusing the chair he held for her, "why did you not investigate that John person's background as I asked you to?"

"I did, my dear," he answered mildly, "and saw no reason to object to his courtship."

"Well you didn't do a very good job of it," she retorted. "Luckily my friend, Tilda, was on the porch of her seamstress's place in one of those dreadful row houses over on University Drive when Mr. McKay came out of the house next door. He actually greeted her. He was followed by a young woman who hugged him, right there in public. What do you think of that, Husband? Your investigation surely fell short. There will be an end to this...now!" So saying, she turned to go, but her husband's arm detained her.

"Wait, my love, there's more to the story. John lives in that row house, with a large family, which includes a young sister. That's probably who Tilda saw."

"He lives there?" Her voice trembled in horror. "Our daughter has been keeping company with a man who lives in a row house? You knew it and did not prevent it? I am undone." Her breath came in short gasps; she fanned herself with her handkerchief.

"My dear, you are not being fair. Many a young man has distinguished himself after a childhood in inferior quarters. I like John. You like John. More to the point, Annie likes John—a lot. Why should he be rejected because he has just arrived and hasn't had time to better himself?"

"Just arrived," gasped his wife. "He's an immigrant? Sir, may I remind you that Annie is an honor graduate of Wesleyan College. Her social standing is impeccable. She can do immensely better than a penniless immigrant. He can't possibly know how to go on. Annie will be shunned by society. Tilda has already mentioned not allowing her daughter at any more assemblies in our home."

"Very well, I will...."

"You will stay out of it. I will take care of this."

Within days John McKay was missing, both from the Anderson home and from the homes of Annie's friends. At church only his eyes spoke to Annie when they met. Finally, one Sunday, he followed her from the classroom, took her by the arm, and pulled her into the empty choir room, shutting the door firmly behind them.

"Annie, I think you know I am desperately in love with you. I cannot bear to be this near, knowing you can never be mine. So I'm moving to New York. Leaving Saturday on the afternoon train. Oh Annie, I shall miss you."

She burst into dismayed tears.

He folded her into his arms. "Father God," he prayed, as her tears soaked his waistcoat, "watch over Annie and give her a good life." He kissed her tenderly, whispered, "Good-bye, my love," and was gone, leaving her sobbing into her dainty handkerchief.

Passing Judge Anderson in the church hallway, John whispered, "Judge Anderson, Annie needs you. She's in the choir room."

What the Judge said to his daughter was never known, but on Saturday her mother found her in her bedroom, packing a suitcase.

"Annie, love, what are you doing?" she enquired.

"Packing," said Annie quietly. "John is leaving, moving to New York. I won't let him go without me. I've prayed about it, and this is my decision."

Before her mother could protest, there was a knock at the open bedroom door. "Excuse me, my dear," said Judge Anderson, "there's someone here to see you and Annie."

Annie's mother glared at the man standing behind her husband. "How dare you elope with my daughter, you fiend," she hissed.

John glanced at the open suitcase and smothered a triumphant grin.

"No ma'am," he said. "I didn't come to elope. I came to tell Annie I've changed my mind. I intend to stay here and prove I am worthy to be your son-in-law, no matter how long it takes."

"Oh, John!" Annie gave a cry of delight and flew into his arms.

In less than a year, Annie and John were married. Judge Anderson gave them the lot next door for a wedding present, and they raised six children in the house they built there. John quickly made a name for himself, in business, in his church leadership, and in the lively social life of Macon, Georgia, where they lived for the remainder of their lives.

John was always thoughtful of his mother-in-law and, when she was widowed, he installed a communication system between the two houses so that she could summon them anytime she needed them.

ANNE MCKAY GARRIS is a retired newspaper editor living in Clearwater Beach, Florida, with her husband, Berle, a retired United States Marine. She enjoys teaching Sunday school, finding seashells on the beach, and hosting Grannie Camp for her children, grandchildren, and great-grandchildren.

# My Country Reward

### * * *

## BARBARA J. BRUNNER

I am a city girl; my husband, Chris, is unquestionably a country boy. Chris was the secondborn of 11 children; I was the baby of four. Chris grew up in a poor family; mine was rather well-to-do. When his family was getting holiday food baskets from local churches, my dad was buying my mother fur coats and convertibles. When Chris and his 10 brothers and sisters were using an outhouse and sharing a canvas bathtub set up in the living room filled with water heated from the wood-stove for their weekly baths, I was enjoying a warm, cozy fire in our family room with a fully-stocked bar and ping-pong table in our beautiful home with three bathrooms. When Chris, as a teenager, was changing diapers for all his younger brothers and sisters and running trap line in the creek before school, I was enjoying summers on our yacht at Lake Erie or swimming in our backyard pool.

Chris hated school and barely graduated. I was an A/B student who loved learning. My children tell me I should have been an English teacher; Chris's language includes "agin the wall," "over yonder," and "britches." Our upbringing and childhoods could not have been more different; however, in the important things in life that matter—our faith in God, our morals and beliefs, our desire to help others—we could not be more alike.

Chris lived his entire life in the country, in Ohio. I am a city girl from Ohio. When I was 12, my dad moved us to Florida, where I eventually married my high-school sweetheart. Twenty years later I returned alone to Ohio with three small children, ages three, eight, and nine. My divorce immediately plunged our family into poverty, where we stayed for the next 10 years. It was extremely hard for all of us; it was exhausting for me. Little did I know that the real trials (as well as the real blessings) were ahead.

My first marriage was so bad—who in their right mind would do that twice? So I promised myself I would never marry again. And for the next 23 years I kept that vow, as I was busy working full-time, being mom and dad to my own children, five foster children, and my grandson.

At 47, I had raised my children and was working to finally realize my dream of finishing college. But when my older daughter had to be hospitalized because of her crippling mental illness, I got legal custody of my five-year-old grandson, Alex. I remember saying, "Wow, I'll be 60 years old when I stop raising children!" I tried unsuccessfully to continue college, because when this little boy's world had just been turned upside down, he needed the only stable person in his life, his grandma. So I dropped out of college, once again.

Alex was a challenge to raise. Because of what he had experienced in his young life as his mother battled schizophrenia, Alex had more "baggage" than the foster children who had lived in my home. He was defiant, rebellious, aggressive, did not follow rules, and did not get along with other children. Because of many confrontations with neighbors, I later decided it was time to move out of our neighborhood. So I reluctantly sold my beloved home, which had been an answer to prayer 16 years earlier, and on a very cold day in February 2001, we moved into a little country home 15 miles outside of town. Little did I know that all of this was part of a bigger plan that included a stranger who lived across the road.

It would be another year before I would meet that stranger. While visiting a nearby church one Sunday, a woman asked if I knew that my neighbor, Chris, was a member there. She pointed him out to me, "He's the guy with the Amish-style beard."

I later introduced myself. "I think I'm your neighbor."

He replied, "I know."

I thought, *This guy's not very friendly.* I learned, however, that when he had recently retired, his wife of 35 years walked out on him, and he was not doing well.

We both attended the adult Sunday school class for yet another year. When the pastor asked for volunteers to open their homes for Bible studies, I was surprised that Chris chose mine. For several months he faithfully came each week, bringing homemade gingerbread or Jello salad. When the Bible study ended, he asked if he could take Alex fishing, knowing that Alex (who was then 11), needed a male influence in his life. I readily agreed.

Their plans to go fishing the next weekend were interrupted when Alex was sent to detention for getting suspended from his school bus. Instead, Chris asked if I would like to get an ice cream. I thought, *Why not? He's a nice Christian man, and we could be friends.*

We went to a little ice cream shop, got a cone and a table, and sat and talked for quite awhile. Chris did most of the talking, telling me about his recent divorce, and like a good friend, I listened. We never considered that a date; there was no attraction whatsoever for either of us.

On my way to a Memorial Day picnic with a friend and her family the next day, I ran into Chris and invited him to join me. Because he had planned to till our pastor's garden, he was wearing blue jeans, suspenders, and a straw hat. When we got to the picnic, my friend, Connie, just stared at him, and we later laughed when she told me she wondered who the Amish guy was that I had found. After eating, Connie and I watched as this patient, kind man spent the next few hours baiting her grandchildren's fishhooks and even seemed to enjoy himself.

We were engaged within six weeks, and married in six months. Connie was my maid-of-honor. People who had known me for years—including my children—were shocked when I became engaged. It was a whirlwind courtship, but we figured when you get to be our age, hopefully you have become a pretty good judge of character, and there's no time to waste. So on our wedding day, not only did we exchange our wedding vows, but I also exchanged my old vow of never remarrying for allowing God to bless me with a wonderful Christian husband whom He had handpicked just for me.

Alex was happy about our marriage, at first. He had never before had to share me with anyone. Sadly, there were many confrontations between him and Chris. I distinctly remember the first time Alex became physical with Chris and pushed him into the stove. Things escalated from there, and at the advice of Alex's therapist, we filed charges against Alex more than once. Consequently, for several years there was a lot of juvenile court involvement. It was a very demanding situation, dramatically complicated by the never-ending false accusations of abuse that my (paranoid) daughter continually made against Chris and me. It was a nightmare I am glad has finally ended.

Alex is now 21 years old, on his own, and doing quite well. Chris had no idea when he married me what he was getting into, and many men would have walked away. Thankfully, he did not.

Chris is a hard-working, fun-loving, caring, tender, giving, compassionate, godly man, who never meets a stranger. When we enjoy canoeing and bike-riding together, I feel like a kid again. He tells me daily he loves me, opens doors for me, fixes me hot tea, and buys me flowers often. We always hold hands; each day he makes me feel special. I am ever so blessed to call him my husband.

From the world's point of view, we are undoubtedly mismatched. From God's point of view, we were made for each other. Years ago I wouldn't have given Chris a second glance; fortunately as we mature we discover what is important and what is not. Chris has all the important qualities that matter, and everything to make a wife happy.

I thank God for Chris every day. The 35 years prior to meeting Chris were ever so challenging and difficult. What a special blessing he is for the latter part of my life.

"Let us not become weary in doing good, for at the proper time we will reap a harvest (*or reward*) if we do not give up" (Galatians 6:9). As a struggling single mom, I hung on to that Scripture for dear life. Today I tell my husband that HE is my reward.

Recently my daughter-in-law gave us a plaque that reads: *It's Never Too Late to Live Happily Ever After.* What a wonderful reminder that you should never say "never," and that sometimes God saves the best for last!

BARBARA J. BRUNNER says she has a Ph.D. in Life, with a wealth of experiences, gleaned knowledge, and wisdom from which to write. She has written the columns *Newton News* and *Grandparents Raising Grandchildren* in a community newspaper and was a contributing *Opinion Shaper* for her daily hometown newspaper.

barbarajbrunner.blogspot.com

# Bear of a Man

### * * *

### BECKY MCGREGOR

Everyone at work heard my first encounter with Bruce. Derogatory words shouted at a glass-shattering volume. Coworkers expected me to be fired at any minute.

I was building 3-D graphics for a billion-dollar project, which meant learning new hardware and a graphics package that gave me fits. My boss promised a computer, loaded and ready to go. Two weeks passed, and I had nothing but a desk and chair stuck in a cubicle.

Monday, after arriving late, being reminded I'd already missed a meeting, finding no coffee in either machine and facing another day with no computer, I snapped.

I stormed in and out of three different offices before I found out that a manager named "Bruce" handled all the new installations. I marched down the aisle, barged right in, and screamed at the top of my lungs, "You need to get off your butt and get to work. You're holding up everything and there is no excuse for it."

Once I wound down, he said, "Hi, I'm Bruce, and you are....?"

My shoulders slumped, and I studied the pattern in the carpet. I felt like a six-year-old throwing a temper tantrum. I tried to gracefully explain what I needed.

As it turned out, Bruce had given the set-up job to another coworker, who had reported the job completed a week ago. In the end, that coworker was in trouble, Bruce apologized for the man's laziness, and I kept telling Bruce, "Sorry I yelled at you."

It took days for everyone at work to stop rehashing the scene: "Can't believe Bruce took that," "When do you think she'll get fired?" and so forth.

After that notorious introduction and knowing the company prohibited dating fellow employees, here I was, ready for a date with Bruce. What was I thinking?

I stared into the mirror. *Becky, it's just a date. He's a guy providing a meal and a night on the town.*

But if that were true, why had I agonized over every detail of my appearance? I wore a little black dress. High heels added to my six-foot frame and showed off my legs, my best physical feature.

I looked calm on the outside, but inside I was shaking. I told my mirror image that my mind ruled tonight, but as I turned around, my heart laughed.

I heard a car pull up outside, and before the engine turned off, I ran to the front door, waited a heartbeat, and slowly opened it.

With one glimpse, I trembled. How was it possible for a man to look so good? Bruce stood so tall that even in my heels I had to look up to see his eyes—crystal blue with flakes of silver. His sun-bleached hair made me think surfer, but his broad shoulders said football player. A slight smile moved across Bruce's face, dimples emerged, eyes twinkled, and my heart reached for him.

Bruce wore a non-work suit and tie. His smile directed my gaze toward those lips, soft, and accessible, leaving me wanting to kiss him. I turned away quickly, trying to get away from the wanting, while grabbing my purse off the entryway table.

"Hi, Bruce," I said.

"Hi, yourself. Ready to go?" Extending an arm, he said, "I cleaned Maurice for tonight."

"Maurice?"

"Sorry, that's my car. Maurice, meet Becky." He opened the door.

"Maurice, you look as good as your driver."

Bruce shut my door and slid into the sports car. "I have the perfect restaurant picked out."

Small talk continued on the drive to the restaurant. I couldn't help but notice Bruce's gentle hands, his style and grace, all wrapped up in a bear of a man. His manners appeared perfect. Maybe that's why I felt so comfortable with him. It shouldn't be this easy or this relaxed.

As the hostess seated us, I was captivated by the Italian atmosphere. The smell of fresh bread mingled with garlic and pasta, swirled around marble columns, inviting us to sit at candle-lit tables. Going out with Bruce was probably a mistake, but once in a while a girl needs to have fun.

"What looks good? I would order for you, but I bet you'd start yelling at me."

"You are never going to let me live that down, are you?"

"No, it's a great story. It made my mom laugh."

"You told your mom?"

"Sure, she said to tell you that you're her kind of woman."

"How embarrassing."

As dinner progressed, I told him about my family. He told me about his cats. I was surprised how forthcoming he was with personal details. It felt like we were the only two people in the world. April 5th was definitely going into my history book as the best date ever.

"I really don't want this to end." The words flew from Bruce's lips. "What if we go back to my place? You could tell me what you think of the decorating job."

"Maybe. Sure, then we can keep talking. You know you really are different from the typical manager."

"You obviously think all managers are the same."

"Sure, all wrapped up in business, corporation comes first, doing anything to get ahead," I said, my voice leaking disdain.

"Whoa! Maybe being alone is not a good idea."

"No, not you. You're not like that. I can't figure out how you got where you are and stayed human."

"Oh, so it's human you're looking for. Well, if you stay past midnight, then you can see what I turn into."

"Okay, you're on."

Bruce escorted me up to a top-floor, corner unit. The entryway radiated warmth. He guided me through the various rooms; it struck me how each room seemed to have a completely different feel and personality.

"Why don't you come and look at the kitchen, my favorite room? I love cooking. You know those cakes at work that everyone devours at birthdays? Those are mine."

"Are you serious? You cook, your taste in clothes is impeccable, and the condo is gorgeous. Thirty-three years old, never married, no girlfriend." My expression changed from surprise to acknowledgment. "Oh, my gosh, you're gay? That's why I feel so safe with you. That's why I can talk to you so easily. I can't believe I didn't see it." I stop to stare. "So why the date? Am I cover for you? Does anyone else know? Or was I not supposed to figure this out?" The questions poured out of my mouth.

Bruce froze. Then his gaping mouth slowly closed as his eyes started to twinkle and a huge smile spread. In two quick strides, he closed the distance between us and his mouth captured mine, his hands instantly in my hair.

His kiss came as a complete surprise, but his lips felt soft, and he tasted so right. He felt so…so right, like he fit. I snapped back into reality, removed his hands and backed away. "What was that?"

"I believe it's called a kiss."

"Yeah, but gay men don't kiss like that."

"I know. I thought it was the easiest way to stop all the gay references."

"Okay, so you're not gay, but something's got to be wrong." I backed away, shaking my head.

"I have my peccadilloes, but I've never found a woman worth the effort to keep. Women are strange creatures, so much drama, and I never know what they want.

"If that's how you feel, why ask me out?"

"You're different. Not sure what it is about you, but there's something. I wanted to figure you out."

"Sorry I pounded your ego with the gay thing."

"I think my ego can handle it. But I'm not sure my lips have recovered from that kiss."

"Sorry, I kissed you back. I wasn't thinking. You caught me off guard. Believe me, it won't happen again. I think I should head home."

"If you're sure..."

"Oh yeah, I'm sure."

Bruce took me home. Both of us remained quiet during the drive. Our backgrounds were different; yet we'd instantly been comfortable with each other and could talk forever. We even shared the same taste in food, movies, and books.

He pulled up to my curb.

"Thanks for the evening. I'll see myself inside."

As I closed the door, my mind took off in all directions. I couldn't believe he kissed me, or how much I liked it. I needed sleep.

Unfortunately, sleep was the last thing I got. The sun rose to find me sipping tea, thinking of Bruce, realizing I was in love with him.

After that, we secretly dated for six months. After realizing there were no rules against employees being married, I walked down an aisle to marry Bruce. We've endured struggles and triumphs for 21 years now. Yet every time I look into his blue eyes, I am reminded of that first date, first kiss, and the moment I realized I was in love.

BECKY MCGREGOR retired from an engineering career and began writing family stories. Two of her short stories were published in *Let's Talk,* a Florida Writer Association Collection published in 2011 and a story in *The Florida Writer,* a magazine published by FWA.

# Double-Knot

\* \* \*

## BEVERLY W. BAILEY

**M**y fiancé and I stood in our pastor's study surrounded by him, his wife, and assistant pastor. It was Tuesday, May 26, 1964—my birthday, and we were getting married. It was a sunny spring day in Birmingham, Alabama. Larry and I were 21-year-old college students at Samford University, madly in love and not a dime to our names, but we knew what we were doing that day was right.

The following Saturday was our scheduled wedding day. Most of the arrangements had been made. The florist was ready to decorate the front of the wide altar with candelabra and white flowers. The bridesmaids' green and yellow dresses were properly fitted, and the organist and soloist had practiced our selections. The bakery confirmed the cake would be ready on time. Our parents, relatives, and friends were excited about the day we would become husband and wife.

Our wedding was to take place at Parkview Baptist Church, where Larry was part-time Minister of Music. We loved the church, and they loved us.

My parents would be the only ones from my side of the family to attend because no one else could afford to travel from Elizabethton, Tennessee, to Birmingham. But family and friends there had given us beautiful and useful wedding gifts. So, why were we in Rev. Wayne B. Jones' study getting married four days ahead of the wedding date?

During the middle of my sophomore year at Samford University, I had a new roommate. A sophomore just like me, Christine and I met in the library where both of us worked. She had grown up in Birmingham in a sad home life with a hateful stepmother, but her loving dad thought his daughter hung the moon. Living in the dorm gave her much-needed freedom. I had broken an engagement soon after Christmas, so I was eager to experience new beginnings. Although I loved Dawson Memorial, where most of us college kids went to church, I wanted to go to Christine's church. All she did was brag about the youth group and how great it was.

On a Sunday evening, January 1963, I walked into Philadelphia Baptist Church auditorium with Christine where the youth was gathered for choir practice. She introduced me to her friends, but I hardly remembered anyone's name except Larry's. I had just met the most handsome guy I'd ever seen. He was tall with black hair, a great smile, and was a Christian—my basic criteria for the man I wanted to marry. Christine told me all about him later that evening as we sat on our beds in the dorm, giggling over my reaction to this wonderful guy.

Christine and Larry grew up in the church together, so she was thrilled to set me up with a date with him. Before I knew it, I was going with Larry to the Valentine Banquet for the youth group. I felt like I was in a magic land where everything was perfect. Everyone was dressed up; red and white Valentine decorations and flowers were everywhere. Gene and Norma Sample, the leaders, were dedicated, fun-loving Christian leaders. We even double-dated with them later on. It wasn't long before both of us were involved in leading worship music in a mission church nearby, enjoying being together as well as knowing we were joining others in helping build a ministry. We also fell in love.

By June, Larry asked me to marry him, and I had a lovely engagement ring. It was time to go to my home in Elizabethton, Tennessee, see Mama and Daddy and hope they would be just as happy as we were. I was aware Mama had misgivings about our relationship, because neither of us had finished college. Education was important to my parents. Their hopes and dreams were rooted deeply in me, their only child; I was the first on either side to go to college. Larry's parents were apprehensive, too, but they were much more objective.

We drove from Birmingham to Elizabethton for a short weekend, so nervous we both had upset stomachs. Larry and I slowly walked in the back door and into the kitchen. After a couple minutes of introductions, Dad hugged Larry like he was his son. Mama simply stood rooted to the floor, briefly glancing at my ring when I showed it to her. My heart sank.

"I'm glad you got here safely. It's a long way to drive. Do you want something to eat?" she asked.

"Yes, I think we're hungry. I hear you're a wonderful cook. Beverly's bragged a lot about all the great food you grow in the garden. I'm sure everything will be good," Larry replied.

I could feel the tears well up.

I'm not sure how we got through the weekend. Mama slowly warmed to Larry's good humor and sweet spirit. We didn't make any wedding plans.

When Larry and I returned to Birmingham and school, however, we started making plans to marry in December. A surprise trip changed our arrangements.

Mama was determined we should complete another year of college before we married. Dad was more understanding but gave in to Mama's wishes. Both unexpectedly showed up in late summer to meet with Larry's parents and hopefully persuade us to change our minds. It was a tearful, heart-wrenching time, but Larry and I agreed to wait until May.

Mama and I argued during the fall and winter about where we would get married as well as the cost. Larry and I wanted our pastor to marry us in this sweet church in Birmingham where Larry served. He loved directing the choirs and the $25.00 per week would certainly help us begin our life together. Though Mama wasn't happy about us not marrying at home, she began to adjust to the idea. While we were home during spring break, family and friends gave us a bridal shower.

School and family problems were stressful on both of us while trying to finalize wedding plans. We were frazzled. As the time grew closer to our May wedding date, we began wonder how we could make our vows more meaningful. What could we do to shut out family and school distractions and focus on God? What did we want to say as we committed our lives to each other and to God for the rest of our days? We decided to have another conference with our pastor whom we loved so dearly.

Rev. Wayne Jones was young himself. He and his wife, Betty, had been married only a few years and had a daughter. On a Sunday evening after church services, we sat in his office and explained our dilemma and frustrations.

The first thing he did was give us a big grin and tell us he loved us. We immediately felt peace. In his counsel he assured us God would provide direction. We asked if he would marry us privately and secretly on Tuesday before our wedding on Saturday. He agreed. We prayed together, all of us in tears.

On Tuesday, I slipped out of the dorm room without Christine suspecting anything, and Larry picked me up in his blue Mercury. I dressed in a beautiful white lace blouse and white skirt with white heels. Larry wore his black suit. We held hands as we rode to the church, both of us crying.

Around 11:00 that morning, Pastor Jones, his wife, Betty, and the assistant pastor, Rev. Don Robison, stood with Larry and me in his study, ready to listen to the words from the Bible that would guide our lives. Besides the traditional vows, we added the beautiful passage from Ruth 1: "Entreat me not to leave thee..." Through tears, we said our vows and prayed. With lots of hugs from Pastor Jones, Betty and the assistant pastor, we left and Larry drove me back to the dorm. So much to do before Saturday and my parents were not even arriving until Thursday.

The four days passed quickly. With God's guidance and help, Mama and Dad and I didn't get into any arguments, nor did I tell them I was married. The wedding and reception were beautiful. The words from one of our musical selections, "Whither Thou Goest," echoed our earlier vows.

Larry and I told no one of our real wedding day for more than 20 years. However, the commitment we made May 26, 1964, and the love and wisdom of a caring pastor were cords "double-knotted" by God. They have held us close through the ups and downs of married life for 48 years.


BEVERLY W. BAILEY is a retired college English professor whose career has also spanned teaching middle-school students and senior citizens. Her son and daughter live nearby, and she has two miracle granddaughters. She and Larry embarked on a new adventure in 2008: They are now certified organic peach growers, nurturing trees that bear luscious fruit.

# Finding the Courage to Love Again

### * * *

## CHRISTINA RYAN CLAYPOOL

My story begins in the early 1990s, when I was the owner of a shabby chic store. Back then, as a 30-something single mom, it wasn't easy to make ends meet selling the discarded treasures of others. Auctions, flea markets, and garage sales were the way I stocked my vintage shop.

One summer day, I stopped at an estate sale hoping to find a few items to resell. The attached garage of the stately brick home was filled with the earthly goods of an elderly widow.

As she walked toward me, the old woman's fragile condition caused her to lean heavily on a three-pronged cane. She was liquidating over a weekend what had taken a lifetime to collect. Her gray hair was disheveled, and her eyes reflected the resignation that must have cost her a great deal.

The widow needed to sell everything and move to a place where she wouldn't be alone. The sale's classified ad didn't say all that, but it didn't take much to figure it out. I decided to buy several items to financially assist her in her season of transition.

"To everything there is a season, and a time for every purpose under heaven...a time to keep and a time to cast away." I had always liked this insightful wisdom from the Book of Ecclesiastes.

But the Bible verses weren't very comforting in light of this woman's heartbreaking circumstances. After all, it was my "time to keep," and her "time to cast away." That's why I let her do all the talking. I never even asked the stranger her name, since she didn't volunteer it.

There was a vintage blouse among her possessions that I selected to purchase, and when the widow saw it, her eyes seemed to look far away. It was as if she was transported to another time. A time when she was young and in love, and her future lay before her.

Decades earlier—I think she said it was the 1940s—the lace top had been part of her wedding attire. Fifty years later, her husband was gone, and she could no longer care for herself. Reluctantly, she gently handed the blouse to me.

I was shocked when the silver-haired senior told me that she had worn the beautiful bodice as a young bride. My original intention was to resell it, but knowing the garment's history now, my plan instantly changed. Before I realized what I was doing, I blurted out, "I promise you that I will keep it always."

I'm not sure whether the aged woman gave me a look of disbelief, relief, or resignation. Her reaction didn't matter. I made a promise, and I intended to keep it. For years, I hung the bodice on a satin hanger displayed with some antique hats on an oak coat rack in the apartment where my young son and I lived.

I never planned on wearing it, because I thought my days of being a bride were over. I tried to tell myself that I had a full life, with my business, my writing, and my little boy. Besides, I had failed at marriage. Not once, but twice, and I wasn't yet 35.

To explain, my first husband left shortly after our wedding, and my second spouse was unfaithful. I guess everyone knew about his serial philandering, except for me. When I found out, he told me it happened because I didn't make him happy.

No doubt, I had some blame to shoulder for these failures, because with divorce, there is never just one person at fault. Maybe I chose the wrong person to begin with. Whatever the reason, I decided it was best to never marry again.

I didn't date for years, thinking I couldn't make a spouse happy anyway. Being a journalist by training, I also wrote a book about surviving emotional heartbreak, but it didn't include any advice about how to love again.

Then I heard a sermon by a marriage expert explaining that, "We are not called to make another human being happy; that is their responsibility." This set me free from a weighty burden I had shouldered for years.

Shortly after learning this truth, I started dating a man from my church. We became engaged in the fall of 1995. Sadly, I had to cancel our wedding 11 days before it was to take place, when my future groom backed out. The "no dating" rule went back into effect after this new rejection.

Five years later, in October 2000, I met Larry James Claypool through a mutual friend when I was invited to speak at a singles event. By then, I was in my mid-40s and had spent more than a dozen years alone. My son was grown. My store had closed, and I was working as a reporter for a west central Ohio television station.

Larry was a 40-something school administrator who had never married. He believed almost immediately that I was the wife he had almost given up hope of ever meeting. Even though we both felt that it was God's plan that brought us together, I was deeply wounded and fearful of being hurt again.

At first, we were just friends. Initially, Larry invited me to supper, calling several times during a six month period. I didn't intend to go out with him, always using my frantic schedule as an excuse. But one day he phoned, when my health had forced me to resign from my TV job. I was lonely and anxious about the future that afternoon, so I agreed to eat supper the following Friday night, on June 8, 2001.

After that first meal, our friendship grew, and we began to spend time together. Larry was patient and undemanding. I didn't even realize we were dating, until I had already started experiencing feelings for him. Despite all my reservations, I began to fall in love with this handsome soft-spoken bachelor.

Even though we were older, our faith caused us to decide to not have sex before marriage. Then, in January 2002, we began attending premarital classes at a local church. We were not yet engaged but wanted to explore and discuss everything about preparing for marriage.

With more than a dozen other couples, Larry and I freely talked about finances, religion, sex, parenting, in-laws, family values, and a host of other subjects. My fears began to dissolve as this gentle, never-married man patiently shared his hopes, goals, and dreams with me.

On February 9, 2002, I sensed that my devoted suitor was going to propose. That morning, as I dressed for our date, I mustered all my courage. Part of that courage came from the fragile-from-age lace bodice, which represented decades of a marriage that had lasted. Instinctively, I reached for the ivory top I had never worn before, and carefully put it on over an off-white shell. It complemented the long black skirt I was wearing.

Larry surprised me by taking me to one of my favorite places, the Swan House Tea Room in Findlay, Ohio. Our table was the only one that had been elegantly set with antique Moss Rose china dishes. The servers took extra effort making everything beautiful, because Larry let them know beforehand he intended to propose.

What he didn't share with the staff was that the Moss Rose pattern is very special to me, because my late mother gave me my own Moss Rose tea set some years earlier.

That Saturday afternoon, Larry knelt before me on one knee and held out a solitaire diamond ring. Then, while smiling broadly, he asked me to be his wife.

The packed tea house held mostly women patrons, and they all excitedly gazed at the romantic scene. Even the busy waitresses in long white aprons stood motionless waiting for my reply. For a few moments, fear prevented me from answering, and Larry's frozen smile turned to anxious concern. It was as if the entire room breathed a deep sigh of relief when I finally said, "Yes." Then it filled with congratulatory applause and joyful laughter.

Our wonderful wedding on June 8, 2002, would have been glorious enough for Cinderella and her prince.

After being married for more than a decade, I will admit that there have been some difficult days. Yet the rewards of finding true love outweigh the struggles. The lace blouse remains in our home, displayed with the antique hats. It is now a reminder of Larry's tea room proposal, coupled with the memory of another woman's long-ago wedding day.

Unfortunately, I will never know that bride's name, although I will be forever grateful that she allowed me to share her ivory bodice. Somehow, with God's grace, the delicate lace top gave me the courage to risk loving again. I'm so thankful, because, most of the time, we truly are living happily ever after.

CHRISTINA RYAN CLAYPOOL is the 2011 First Place National Amy Writing Awards winner, a Christian speaker, and author. She has been featured on CBN's *700 Club* and Joyce Meyer Ministries, and is married to Ohio public schools superintendent, Larry Claypool.

www.christinaryanclaypool.com/blog/1
www.christinaryanclaypool.com

# The Plan

### * * *

## CINDY M. JONES

A t 18, I wanted to die. I tried my best to carry out my plan of suicide, but it didn't work.

My father died when I was only 12 and, with him, my wonderful childhood. My life became more and more bleak, until one day I couldn't take it anymore.

My plan was simple. Walk to the end of our dusty clay road in rural Mississippi, wait for a lumber truck to speed around the sharp 90-degree turn, jump, and die.

After writing good-bye and apology letters, I set out to end it all. Halfway there, I heard a voice calling my name. It was familiar, yet I couldn't place it.

"Hello, is anyone there?" I asked. Seeing no one, I thought, *I must be losing my mind.* Speeding up, I heard the voice a second time. Every fiber in my body stiffened. I ran toward my end.

*"Cindy."* The voice, more gentle this time, flowed through my whole being.

"Yes, Lord," I said. I hadn't heard that voice in seven long, lonely years. The same voice said three times, *"I have a plan for you."*

Back home, I tore up the notes, began reading my Bible, prayed (a lot), and never considered suicide again. Hope for something good was possible again. God had kept me from killing myself that day, but why and what was "the plan"?

Exactly three months later, someone knocked on our back door. It was after midnight. "Who in the world could be knocking on the door at this hour?" I said out loud to no one in particular. Opening the door, I stared back into the deepest pools of sky blue that I'd ever seen.

"Can I please use your phone?" he asked. "My name is Bryan. I've just had an accident." He explained that he was new in town, had taken a wrong turn, and landed in a ditch not far from my home.

"Who will you call? No one will be up," I told him.

We walked down the road to where he had lost control of his car, a red Trans Am. A full moon gave us plenty of light, and the stars glittered like Christmas. A crisp breeze blew my hair, taking my breath away.

He reached over and took my hand. "Cold?"

His kind demeanor, the way he cared, made me shiver, and I didn't believe it was the damp foggy air.

We stopped in a spot I knew well. I couldn't believe it. It was the same spot God had spoken to me months earlier.

My uncle pulled up beside us. "I heard the commotion. Need help?"

The following day Bryan knocked on my door again, "Just wanted to thank you." His blue eyes, more vivid in the sunshine, fascinated me. His smile made my heart flip-flop. I knew him, from somewhere, before. He kept coming, weekend after weekend, until Christmas Eve.

He introduced me first to his mom, then to the rest of his family sitting around the dining room table at his aunt's house.

"I brought you this." I placed the floral and candle arrangement in front of his mom.

"It's beautiful." She pulled me into a deep hug. I had almost forgotten what that felt like. "I want to show you something," she said. Picking up a photo album, she turned several pages. "There." She tapped her finger on a picture. "Do you remember that day?"

It was a picture of a small blond boy wearing nothing but a diaper saddled on my pony, Mandy. She went on and tapped another picture. It was me standing by my pony with the blond boy.

"Why do you have a picture of me and Mandy?" I asked.

"It was the day your daddy bought Bryan's pony for your birthday," she said, grinning. "The day before we moved."

The plan was to finish something that felt over and done with... my life. The plan became a beginning instead of an ending.

Bryan and I dated for two and a half years before he proposed. We've moved some 23 times, meeting many people that became dear friends.

Because his profession took us to so many places, we decided that we would homeschool our children. Our local homeschool co-op needed help teaching. Teaching reading classes, creative writing classes, and an American Girl's club became some of the best days of my life. A fellow homeschooling mom introduced us to soccer for my oldest son, Daniel. "It will help him get over his shyness," she said.

Not long after Daniel began soccer, a coach came up to my husband after a game. "He's got a talent for this," he said.

That became my husband's cue. He personally undertook the job of perfecting my son's skills, then our younger son's skills, and lastly our daughter's skills. Thousands of games, hundreds of players, and 15 years later, what began as a hobby developed into our ministry. We coached, we encouraged, we took care of, and became involved in many of the lives of our players as well as their parents. Each roster, from each season—all 15 years of them—is still in our filing cabinet and serves as a reminder to pray for each one.

To entertain my children, I began making up stories from growing up. I wrote them down not to forget and soon was writing lots of things: lists, journal entries, curriculum, newsletter articles, newspaper articles, and magazine articles. Hearing that inner voice to tell my story, I knew God's plan was unfolding.

As I write and speak to groups now, I tell them how God spoke to me the day I wanted to end my life. Using my story, I've been able to talk with abused teens. It never amazes me that the very ones I am ministering to want to take my hand and tell me how sorry they are. "I can't believe you went through all that, and well, you seem so normal and happy," one teen told me after I had given my testimony. "Does that mean things will be okay for me too?"

"If God can do it for me, he can do it for anyone," I say.

Daily I'm overwhelmed by God's goodness, grateful for the many opportunities to be a blessing to those around me, and indebted to him for transforming my plan into his plan, which is perfect.

Recently I visited home. Mom still lives on that same dusty, red, clay road in Mississippi. Turning down onto it in the sharp curve sends chills all through my nervous system like an icy induced brain freeze. The point where the road turns up and dips down, I press on the brakes.

*"I have a plan for you."* The words soar through my heart, and I forget why I ever wanted anything other than what I have now.

CINDY M. JONES'S articles have appeared in *Thriving Family, Journey Devotional for Women, Birmingham Magazine, Birmingham Business Journal, Birmingham Parent,* and *The Old Schoolhouse.* Cofounder of Cahaba Christian Writers, she is an avid teacher and speaker. Cindy and her husband live in Birmingham.

http://www.cindymjones.com/

# Love in Three-Quarter Time
## Helen and Ben's Story

*** ***

### DEANNA HOETKER HURTUBISE

Helen ran to make a human barrier between her enraged, drunken father and her terrified mother, something she found herself doing nearly every weekend from childhood to young adulthood. A successful printer, Lou stayed sober during the work week, but Fridays marked the beginning of the family secret, the two days of hell for Helen, her two brothers, and her downtrodden mother. It was the Great Depression and Nell, having married at the age of 18, had no marketable skills to permit her to leave her incurably alcoholic husband to support three children on her own. She remained endlessly trapped in predictable, migraine-filled weekends.

From childhood on, when Helen left school on Friday afternoons, she stopped in to church and begged God to let this weekend be different. But the prayer was never answered. By age 22, her mantra became, "Marriage? Who needs it?" She had fallen in love once or twice but always managed to end the relationship, to the dismay of her confused suitors, before they had an opportunity to pop the question…until Labor Day weekend, 1932.

Every Saturday and Sunday, guys and gals boarded the paddle wheeler on the Ohio River boat landing, heading to Moonlight Gardens Dance Pavilion at Coney Island. Helen and her girlfriends stepped on board that Sunday night to the familiar music of the calliope, ready to fill their dance cards one last time before the summer ended. Ben and his younger brother, Al, whom Helen knew from school, did the same, knowing that this holiday weekend would be the last for a while to swing and sway to the infectious music of the Big Band.

Ben, one of 13 children of German immigrant parents, worked hard during the week to help support his family during those hard times and spent the little extra money he had for admission to a night of music, dancing, and girl watching. His reputation for being an excellent dancer ensured that no girl ever refused his name on her dance card.

That night, his eyes went right to a beautiful brunette, petite and curvaceous, with big blue eyes that seemed to have endless depth. They were beautiful eyes, he thought, but a bit haunting as well; they seemed to look right through him. Helen's attention immediately went to Al and the tall, lanky, Lincolnesque guy with the square jaw, the cleft chin, and the blondish, wavy hair that had a mind of its own. He had a hearty laugh that filled the room, and she knew she needed Al to introduce her.

After polite introductions and casual, flirtatious conversation, Ben extended his hand and asked if he could sign her dance card. There were several names ahead of his, but Ben hardly took his eyes off her while he waited his turn.

Several songs later, Helen was waiting for her next partner to show up, and Ben saw his opportunity. He was at her side in seconds asking, "Where is your partner for this song?" Staring into his pale, blue eyes, she replied, "I don't know; he must be delayed." Then, to her total amazement, Ben took her card, tore it up and said, "Well, this music is too good to waste!" After that initial waltz, during which they laughed, talked, and fit together like they had been partners forever, Ben and Helen's love awakened in ¾ time, and no one else ever signed her dance cards again.

At the end of the evening, Ben walked her to the waiting paddle wheeler. She blushed when he said, "I think September 3, 1932 has been my lucky night."

They dated every week for the next six months and, to her surprise, Helen's father took a real liking to Ben, something he had never done with any other suitor. When Ben casually mentioned that her father seemed like a nice enough man, her emotional response was, "I knew you were a charmer, but this time you must be a snake charmer!"

Seeing his confusion when he pressed for an explanation, she finally felt comfortable enough to share her family secret with him. Ben's heart broke as he listened to her describe a scenario he could hardly imagine—the weekend reigns of terror that were so totally different from the noisy, fun, family dynamic he'd grown up knowing. He embraced her as she cried and said, "Oh, Honey, My Honey, I had no idea."

By Easter, 1933, when he proposed, Ben had worn down Helen's wall of mistrust and fear of marriage. For the next 68 years, he never called her Helen; she was always introduced as "My Honey."

Grateful for the love they found, they chose Thanksgiving Day for the beginning of their life together. At the wedding reception, the newlyweds waltzed to the familiar song, "Oh, How We Danced on the Night We Were Wed." The only thing that marred the day for Helen was the nagging fear of what would happen to her mother on the weekends without her there for protection. One of Helen's brothers had died early of a heart attack, and the other did nothing to help her mother. Eventually, after Nell suffered two heart attacks, Ben and Helen brought her to their home to live her remaining years in love and safety. Nell never laid eyes on her abuser again, and Ben became her son. But that wasn't so surprising since he loved Nell and his Honey enough to do anything for them.

Their lives together were spent in hard work, building a business, and bringing up two daughters, but they never stopped dancing together. Every weekend, they played records on their Hi Fi and danced to the Big Bands in their living room. Saturday nights, if they had no social plans, they turned on *Lawrence Welk* on the TV and danced to his bubbly music. Members of several social dance clubs, they continued this mutual interest well into their golden years. Waltzing into their 70s, 80s, and 90s, Ben and Helen were always the last ones to leave the dance floor. It was evident that, when their bodies moved in sync, to them it was still September 3, 1932. The magic never left.

Their last dance was at their granddaughter's wedding reception in 2001. Guests, both young and not so young, watched them through eyes of admiration as the oldest guests on the dance floor never missed a beat.

A month later, at the age of 96, Ben died of a ruptured aneurism. As all the family members gathered tearfully around his bed in the ER to say good-bye, the priest finished giving the last rites and asked Helen what she was thinking, as she seemed very far away.

She answered wistfully, "I was thinking of the lyrics to one of the songs we loved to dance to." When the priest asked her what they were, she responded, "I'll be seeing you in all the old familiar places."

How could she say good-bye to the only man who ever allowed her to trust, to believe in the promise of a happy marriage and had provided just that for over six decades?

Helen, my mother, lived for five more years with me and my husband, sleeping in the same white, French Provincial bed she and Ben had bought when they married in 1933. Every night, she propped herself up on several pillows and wrote him a note about her day and how much she missed him. There were songs she could no longer listen to, and a good book took the place of her TV on Saturday nights. Those were lonely years, despite all our efforts to make her happy. She'd smile when she was with her seven grandchildren and 11 great-grandchildren or whenever she found herself in social situations she couldn't avoid, but the light had gone out of those deep, blue eyes.

Then in 2006, after a struggle with pneumonia, her time without my father came to an end just weeks before her 96th birthday. Unbelievably, in the wee hours of September 3rd, exactly 74 Labor Day weekends after they shared their first waltz, I am convinced that Ben returned in the hush of night to sign his Honey's card one more time and led her to a Heavenly dance floor for all eternity.

DEANNA HOETKER HURTUBISE is a retired high school French language teacher. Wife, mother of three, and grandmother of eight, she is the author of three children's books: *So Many Hugs, The Boys Who Discovered Yesterday,* and *A Guardian Angel's Lesson.* She and her husband live in Cincinnati.

To email her: **maddiesmeme@yahoo.com.**

# Engaged by Accident

* * *

## DELORES CHRISTIAN LIESNER

I'd never have thought I'd get my dream marriage proposal AFTER I was married, but it was bound to happen to a couple who got engaged by accident!

Ken said he always wanted to meet someone new "by accident," and on September 10, 1961, he got his wish.

I'd moved to Racine that June to join my sister, Marlene, and that fall we were both invited to weddings back home. The cheapest mode of transportation those days was train or bus, but little did we realize that both were about to be affected by major strikes, and we would not have a way home.

Our dad offered to drive us back and return to work the following morning, but the thought of him chain-sawing trees the next day after no sleep nixed that idea. The only mode of transportation left that could get us back to work on time was a plane. Panic does not make for clear thinking—at least in our family—so we quickly booked the airline tickets, without realizing the plane would land 35 miles from home.

We'd packed identical outfits because, although I was 17 and underage, my sister at 21 was often mistaken as my twin, and we'd discovered we could stay out after curfew by having Marlene drive so she would be the one asked for ID when we were stopped. It worked beautifully. I only got a flashlight glare and never was asked for proof of my age. As long as we were going on a plane, we decided to play it up, and wore striped blazers and shoes Ken swears looked like something stolen from Santa's elves.

It was a blast. Marlene ordered an alcoholic drink, gave her ID, and I simply said, "Make that two." Thus our first experience in the air delivered two giddy dressed-alike and almost look-alike sisters to Mitchell field in Milwaukee.

First things first, so we explored every shop and restaurant and arcade—as excited as any first-time traveler to a foreign land, which it seemed like to us country girls. It was only after we picked up our baggage that it occurred to us we needed a ride home. Frantic phone calls and suspicious mothers ruled out anyone we'd met in the Milwaukee area. Marlene's friend Jon from Racine knew that his friend, Ken, had a car and might be willing to come get us. The pay phone's ringing a few minutes later assured us that Jon, Ken, and another friend, Don, were on their way and would meet us by the escalator. There was an escalator? I'd never been on one before.

That's where Ken found me—going up and down the escalator one last time.

"They're here," Marlene informed me, and I turned to see three grinning fellows looking up from the bottom of the moving stairs. I recognized Marlene's friend, and of the other two, I said, "I think I'll marry that one," pointing to Ken—tall and slim, wearing a white dress shirt, jeans, and black dress shoes with white sport socks.

The fellows invited us for a snack at a nearby restaurant that had tiny booths that fit either two or four. Jon, Marlene, and I slid into one of the four-person booths, then Ken and Don did the "go ahead"—"no, you go ahead" routine until we weren't sure if both wanted to sit next to me, or neither.

Finally Ken said he'd sit there, and slipped into a half-booth across the aisle, facing us. I felt him watching me, but each time I'd catch him looking at me, he'd quickly and shyly duck his head toward the food. Between talking to the others, I'd try to catch a glimpse of him as well, so he knew I returned his interest.

He got up quickly when we went to leave and ushered me to the car, so I sat next to him in the front, and Marlene, feeling protective, slid in the front as well, leaving Jon and Don in the back.

The sputtering of the car a few minutes later let us know that Ken forgot to fill up the tank before they left Racine to pick us up. It was dark by then, and the back seat boys offered to go find gas so Ken could stay and protect the ladies.

Once we were on the road again, Ken and I moved to adjust the radio at the same time, and our hands touched. Electricity! I wondered if that was really how Edison discovered it.

Though Ken said he'd like to see me again, he did not call for a week. I finally gave up and "gussied up" in gold. Gold clothing, gold-sprayed hair, and painted nails made quite a sight as I entered the movie theater.

Midway into the movie, I was called to the office for an emergency phone call. It was my sister, saying, "Gasp, like you are in shock." As I obeyed, she explained that she was at a party and Ken wanted to come get me. As I waited outside, I realized what I was wearing, and when he arrived, I saw his eyes widen. I asked if he'd like me to stop home and change, and he readily agreed.

We saw each other almost daily after that, frequently walking near the lake and past the downtown stores. One Saturday night a month later, I had my hair in rollers when Ken called and suggested a walk.

I tied a scarf over the bristled curlers. We parked the car downtown and walked to the beach. On the way back to the car we passed a jewelry store with a very gaudy $29 set of rings featured in the window display. We were laughing and joking that for only $29 a couple could begin a new life together, when the door opened and a sales lady asked if she could show us anything.

Ken raised his brows at me, and I gamely said, "Sure, the sparkly $29 set in the window!" Of course we both felt it was too gaudy, and I expected to leave as she removed the set from my hand, but she turned to Ken and asked if he would like to see some simpler rings. His quiet agreement shocked me.

Stunned, I continued to try on various rings, until the clerk apologized that the store was about to close. I sighed with relief, thinking, *We have an excuse to end our "game,"* but she again turned to Ken, asking, "Would you like to hold any of these on layaway?"

I almost fainted when he said, "Yes" and pointed to the single diamond and gold band I still wear today—49 years later.

We walked out of the store in stunned silence. We were both apparently asking ourselves what had just happened. *Did we just get engaged?* We talked about anything else on the way home, and it wasn't until the beginning of December that Ken told me the rings were off layaway. He gave me the ring December 4th, and we were married the following April.

We had a lovely wedding and honeymoon, which included an accidental side-trip to the Kentucky Derby, where we were invited out of the rain to sit in box seats with Colonel Sanders. It wasn't until four months later, when a coworker came in starry-eyed, sharing her morning proposal, that I realized I'd never been asked.

I headed home, determined to prove our engagement wasn't just an accident.

Though I had to agree with Ken that it was a little late, he still got down on his knee that night, and laughingly asked, "If we hadn't gotten accidentally engaged, would you still have married me?"

Though I'd already affirmed at our wedding months prior our belief that we were meant to be together, the giggly belated enactment confirmed our agreement with a quote by Friedrich Schiller: "There is no such thing as chance; and what seem to us merest accident springs from the deepest source of destiny."

DELORES CHRISTIAN LIESNER exuberantly experiences life in Racine, Wisconsin, as God's delivery girl. She writes the "21st Century Grandma" column for *Prime* magazine, the blog *Look What God Has Done* at **http://deloresliesner.com**, and has published hundreds of articles and stories in anthologies, magazines, and on the internet.

# A Shining Example of True Love

### * * *

## DIANA LEAGH MATTHEWS

Growing up as children, we were frequently embarrassed by our parents. We didn't want to go out in public with them while they held hands. In retrospect, we were very lucky to have parents who truly loved one another and were not ashamed to express their feelings. They were never ashamed to share a kiss or embrace in front of us children. Even when circumstances were difficult, we always knew our parents loved one another.

Mama and Daddy met while in high school. He was a senior, and she was a sophomore. The two of them shared a study hall class together. Daddy was usually very quiet, but apparently he saw something in Mama. Enough that he would often pick on her and give her a difficult time. All of it was done in good fun, such as telling the teacher she didn't go to study hall.

Two years passed before their paths crossed again. Daddy was several hours away at college, and Mama was a senior in high school. On May 16, 1970, Mama made plans with his sister to play putt-putt. Daddy was coming home from college that weekend, and he and his cousin decided to tag along. Neither one had any idea that their lives would head in a new direction that evening. While playing putt-putt, they sensed an attraction to one another. Things evolved from there as the two of them caught up with one another. They always considered this to be their first date. Before the night was over, Daddy asked her to go on a date with him.

They had a lot of dates with his sister and cousin accompanying them. Their first date alone was to the movies where they saw *Oklahoma!* After the movie they went to Howard Johnson's for supper.

On the Fourth of July they made plans to go for a picnic after Daddy got off work. That day ended with a downpour, and they had their picnic under an umbrella at a local park.

When the fall semester arrived, Daddy was sad to tell her good-bye. He returned the four hours away to college. He did not have the finances to come home very often. He and Mama would write letters to each other. He made arrangements with a supervisor to call her from the college switchboard on Friday evenings where they would talk for hours.

Mama says she knew immediately that Daddy was the one she would marry. She'd dated other boys before, but never felt about these boys the way she immediately felt about Daddy. The facts that her parents liked him and she was a friend of his sister's were also bonuses. Both were followers of Christ and shared the same beliefs. Apparently it took him a little longer to realize she was the one, but not too long. They were discussing marriage pretty early in their relationship.

One weekend in October, Mama and her parents went to visit him at college. Her parents were in the back seat of the car, and they stopped for gas. Mama was standing outside with him when Daddy said, "What if we name our firstborn Edward Bruce, after both of our fathers?"

Mama was left speechless. After all, this was the first time he'd mentioned the future in such a specific way.

When Valentine's Day rolled around, Daddy planned to propose. They had already been to the jewelry store and picked out her engagement ring. He came home to spend the weekend with his sweetheart. Apparently he was too excited to wait until Valentine's Day.

On Friday evening, two days before Valentine's, he wrapped his arm around Mama. At the time he was driving and she was on his bench seat beside him. While going around a corner, he asked, "Will you be mine forever?"

Although Mama knew he planned to propose, she was pleasantly surprised when he did pop the question. That evening when she told her parents, her mom playfully slapped her. Not because she didn't like Daddy, but because she was surprised they were getting married so quickly. Actually, Daddy was the only guy she dated that her parents did like and approve of.

Mama and Daddy planned to wait two years until Daddy finished college to marry. However, they eventually decided to move the wedding up a year. After 15 months of engagement, they were married on May 26, 1972. She'd always said that she was probably the calmest one at the wedding. They were married on Daddy's 22nd birthday.

In later years Daddy would tell everyone that he married Mama to have her mama as his mother-in-law. His Mama had always been ill, and his mother-in-law filled the void of having a mama that was left. Life wasn't always easy, especially in those early years. Daddy was finishing school and working to support a wife. Still, they were together and happy.

Over the years they added three children to the family. Daddy went on to seminary and together they pastored several churches together. There were a number of storms and hard times throughout the years, but they always got through things together. They were very different, but their relationship worked; they were able to balance one another.

Years later, Daddy discovered he had cancer. He put up a valiant fight, while Mama stayed by his side. She spent the nights in the hospital and went with him for his treatments. We were all hopeful that he would beat the disease, but it was not to be. Twenty-eight years after they were married, Mama was left a widow. Two of their children were still teenagers in the home. She did everything she could to care for her family and raise her children. This wasn't easy, missing Daddy so much, but she did an amazing job.

Mama always said that Daddy treated her like a porcelain doll, and she knew how precious she was to him. After his death, she discovered strength and resilience she never realized was there. She had no choice but to carry on and provide for their family.

Daddy has been gone for over a decade, but he's still greatly missed. Mama remembers all of their anniversaries and fondly shares some of her memories with us children. They were far from perfect, but they had the type of love we all long to find.

DIANA LEAGH MATTHEWS is a proud daughter of the love her parents shared. She is a vocalist, writer, speaker, and genealogist who shares the love of Jesus through her powerful story. You can find out more about her and read her blogs at:

**www.dianaleaghmatthews.com**
**www.alookthrutime.com**

# James' Heart

\* \* \*

## ELIDA S. VINESETT

In the summer of 1958, at age 16, I walked to my first job at the neighborhood grocery store in South Norfolk, Virginia. The thought of money in my pocket put a spring in my step the entire eight blocks.

James and I became aware of each other at about the same time. He had a ruddy complexion and sported a blond crew cut. While he burned cardboard at the back of Be-Lo Market, he watched me stroll towards him, a skinny Puerto Rican with long black hair that swung from a ponytail. I sensed his stare of my every movement but paid no attention until I noticed how cute he looked. Embarrassed, I murmured, "Hi."

He flashed a mischievous grin, also said "Hi," and followed me inside. I did not know that he, the assistant butcher, would work alongside me in the meat department.

James, an affable, yet cocky 17-year-old, tried to get me to notice him, despite the fact I acted aloof to all his efforts. That daily scenario tickled Peggy, the meat wrapper. She knew my strict parents did not permit their two older daughters to date, except to go with each other to the local community dances. Always cautious, we knew better than to encourage any flirtations from the boys.

Although sheltered, we could earn money during summer vacations. I packaged poultry and beef and washed the blood-spattered pans. Later, my schedule changed to end at 10:00 p.m.

James asked, "Hey, Leda, do you mind if I walk you home? I pass by it every work day." Required to be on his feet all day in the store, he didn't complain that he had to hike an additional 14 miles from home and back.

Born in Gaffney, South Carolina, he walked everywhere, even to Charlotte, which took an hour to reach by car. James, one of 11 kids, often rebelled against his parents' attempts to keep him home and out of trouble. With not much to do in a small mill town, he grabbed the first opportunity to get out and now lived with his sister's family in Virginia Beach.

Soon we knew we had fallen in love. Each time he accompanied me home, the small vineyard in my backyard became our private spot, seen by no one. I chose to ignore Dad's warning: "I don't want any boys calling or coming to this house."

Thus, telling fibs about my whereabouts to spend more time with James became the norm. We would hop on a bus to watch a movie or enjoy the city park. From time to time, he borrowed his brother-in-law's motorcycle, and we headed towards the amusement center at the beach. In one gaudy gift shop, James asked, "Do you want a souvenir with our names engraved on it?"

I nodded, and he bought a pendant and a chain for one dollar. The heart-shaped metal trinket, his first name on one side and mine on the other, hung around my neck as we smiled at one another. The news of my treasure or the fact a boyfriend existed could not be shared with anyone. It saddened me to keep a secret about my first true love. I felt safe with James. He could make me laugh at any time and never raised his voice in anger. James did get into fist fights with other boys before coming to Virginia and committed other shenanigans, but his normally easygoing outlook on life fascinated me.

The next day at school, the necklace felt secure under my blouse, and I tried not to show the happiness I felt when classmates approached to chatter about the upcoming dances. The Junior prom and the Senior dance were special events I could attend with men at least 21 years old. Dad, a retired sailor, knew the unwanted consequence of sexual attacks on minors made them safer dates. So he held the rape charge card in his upper sleeve. He also told them that he kept a loaded shotgun in the house.

For almost two years, James and I continued to date, yet never went beyond the kiss-and-don't-tell sessions. After high school graduation, college life made it impossible to see my boyfriend for weeks. Three months into the semester, he telephoned and hoped his girl would answer this time.

"Did you go to class today?" he asked. "I tried to find you in all the buildings, but no luck."

Puzzled, I explained, "Another asthma attack. Why were you at the college?"

He paused, then answered, "Because...we're getting married tomorrow."

After a few seconds of stunned silence, he revealed his crazy plans. Still, it sounded good to me. If I could not date, I might as well get married.

The next day, my car pool, full of female college students, dropped me off in downtown Norfolk. Denied a reason for the revised routine, the gossip would start with the final wave good-bye.

In anticipation, James searched for me at the Greyhound bus station. The instant he saw me, he beamed and drew near. "Let's find rings at a jewelry store near here." A short time later, we made our selections, and James paid $25, half of his weekly salary.

Pleased with ourselves, I clung to his arm as we hurried back to the depot and chose a secluded bench. When he gently clasped my hands, I whispered, "You need to propose to me in the right way."

With a look of surprise, James cleared his throat and asked in a low, sincere tone, "Leda, will you marry me?"

"I don't know—I'll have to think about it some more." Then I giggled.

He laughed at my tease. Neither of us felt unsure about the elopement. It seemed like the natural thing to do.

We boarded a bus to Elizabeth City, North Carolina, because Virginia law in 1960 stated that those under 21 needed parental consent. We enjoyed the 70-mile trip and, a few hours later, became excited to see the welcome sign to the city. James received information on where to go for the license and the required physical health check. The bus terminal, courthouse, doctor, and the justice of the peace—all established within a three-block area—met the demand for quick marriages. Still, it would take time to complete each step before the final bus departed at 4:30 p.m.

*Where did the hours go?* Less than eight minutes remained to find the local magistrate who would perform the ceremony. After we located him and described our predicament, he grabbed the first witness in the hallway. The wedding vows, recited in record time, did not allow for a single kiss. We clutched our signed certificate and ran all the way to the bus station, where we watched the Greyhound lurch toward the exit out of town.

"James, what are we going to do?" I asked, unable to mask the panic in my voice. Without hesitation, he flagged a taxi, barked directions, and we jumped in back.

*Did we really get married?* I cast an anxious glance at my new husband before he put his arms around me and kissed me. I felt reassured. We kissed throughout most of the ride. The driver kept looking at us in his rearview mirror.

With Norfolk in sight, James suggested, "Leda, I think you should stay with your folks until we know what to do next."

"That's a good idea." I hid my wedding band in my wallet.

It took about two weeks before Dad found out we eloped and confronted me. "You could have married a doctor or even a lawyer," he screamed. "Instead, you married a *chicken* boy!"

Terrified of my dad's explosive temper and his slap-ready leather belt, I called my husband, who came within minutes. We sat in the front living room, braced for the pandemonium to erupt. Mom's soft cries could be heard from the next room; meanwhile, my siblings, too frightened to move, listened.

Dad bellowed, "You don't want her. She's spoiled, selfish, and immature. And she's always sick."

James, with self-controlled patience, waited until his father-in-law had his say. Afterwards, he spoke with confidence and unabashed determination. "We love each other, we are legally married, and I'm taking my wife back with me." We left and disregarded the curse hurled against our success.

Decades later, against all odds, we celebrated our 51st wedding anniversary. Our marriage, later accepted by my parents, proved to be imperfect with the usual problems. However, it endured with God's blessings.

I gaze now at the metal pendant, cool in my hand, and smile. Although it was shiny when new, it is now tarnished and corroded. I would never part with James' *heart,* for it is a reminder that our love today is as beautiful as when his gift was first given.

ELIDA S. VINESETT earned her M.B.A., became a software developer, and began writing with Toastmasters. Married for 51 years, she and James are both retired, living in North Carolina. Elida enjoys family, travel, and T'ai Chi. She believes the joy of the Lord gives her the strength to meet daily challenges.

You may email her at: **vconect@yahoo.com.**

# Perfect Chemistry

\* \* \*

## FREDRICK G. DOLISLAGER

C hemistry always intrigued and challenged me...much like women. As a hopeful college freshmen and pre-med student, I was majoring in Chemistry, Biology, and Natural Science—just to be sure I covered all the bases. I was also avidly perusing a minor in chasing girls. As a budding scientist, it was important to explore the various reactions achievable with different girls. Right? How can you know how strong a bond you have with one girl, if you don't try and replace her with a "chemical" sporting another structure? I tell you, the life of a chemist is tough.

My freshman year was all right. I won the freshman chemistry award and was dating my teacher's niece from a nearby college. In the interest of science, I was also dating a girl who worked at my college. It turns out that double bonds are not a good idea. Just before school was to start for my sophomore year, my professor quit taking his lithium and had a psychotic break. He had a poor interaction with my girlfriend on staff, and she eventually quit and left. At the same time, I lost his niece to some guitar-playing hippie.

Dr. Guy D. Griffin to the rescue. Dr. Griffin accepted the last-minute plea from my college to teach Organic Chemistry for the recently institutionalized professor. "Doc," as I irreverently called him, could only come one night a week. The class lasted three hours. For the first class he brought his daughter to check out my school as a potential college. For three hours she walked past the open classroom door. Back and forth. Back and forth. Gorgeous flowing blond hair, blue eyes, tall, tan, thin, a few sun freckles, and incredible electron orbitals. My minor was about to become my major—and it would take just about as long to achieve.

I can't remember if I spoke to her that evening or not. Doc was an incredible teacher. I thought, *If she's got half his talent, we'll be inseparable.* My classmates and the student-teacher got their laboratory instructions, and away Doc and daughter went. I finished that year of school without seeing her again.

Doc was such a hit; they asked him back to teach my junior year. Now I was the student teacher in charge of the organic lab. Just like last year, he showed up the first evening with his daughter. I got my lab instructions from Doc and then had three hours to focus my attention and considerable intercollegiate skills on Sue. I immediately initiated our first encounter. I didn't ask; I took her to a basketball game on campus. What a great three hours. I found out as much as I could, while being totally cool and aloof: basically she was between (four-year) schools at the moment and taking classes near home. I wondered if she might come to my school since her dad taught here. That might be too much to hope for. As much as I wanted to sustain the reaction with more catalyst, Doc and Sue left.

Upon completion of my junior year, I got an internship at Doc's real job, Oak Ridge National Laboratory. I ended up in a Health Physics lab; I was not only getting paid, but getting one college credit. My first night in town, Doc had me over for dinner. Oh boy! Sue was there! Her mom was normal, house was normal, Doc was normal enough, the cat was normal, and they went to a normal church. Wow, perfect in oh, so many facets of a beautiful crystalline structure derived from a supersaturated solution of wonderful qualities.

Sue was entertaining a girlfriend, but I took every chance I could to wedge between them. Much to my disgust, I found out that Sue was leaving the next day for the whole summer to work at Yellowstone National Park. I was left in a strange town and the only girl I knew was leaving. What type of slow titration is this? Three drops of indicator solution in 2.5 years?

The internship was cool. Today I work with my health physics mentor from way back then. He, unlike Doc, was smart enough not to introduce me to his daughter.

Back to school for my senior year. I was running out of money and petitioned the Dean to give me two credits for my summer internship, instead of one. He gladly accepted, but I had to pay for the extra credit. Doing that meant I could graduate one semester early. But to do so, I had to drop the Chemistry and Biology degrees and just take the Natural Science. Oh, well. I didn't see Sue or Doc that fall as a full-time replacement was found. It would turn out to be my last semester to wander the periodic table of elements: redheads, blondes, and brunettes. Nothing but weak dipole interactions despite senioritis from those seeking a Mrs. Degree.

With graduation looming, I needed a job. My mentor at ORNL said he could hire me for nine months starting in January. Awesome. My first night in town I had dinner at Sue's, with her parents. Dinner was great. I called Sue as soon as I got home. I found some courage and asked her out on a date for the very next day. Before we had our first official date, I had finished college. From that first date on, we saw each other every day for five months—until she went to work at Yellowstone again...for the entire summer.

I learned a lot about chemistry in that time: opposites attract, it takes at least two pure reactants and heat to make a product with greater properties. We were bonded tighter than two carbon atoms in an acetylene molecule. When she returned, she went to my Alma Mater to finish school.

I took her to South Florida for Christmas break to see my folks. While there I called Doc and asked if it would be all right if I asked his daughter to marry me. I was relieved that he said yes. I put a diamond ring on her finger as the sun set over the water at a park on the Intracoastal Waterway.

I made her finish college before I married her, because, you know, the equation of love must be balanced. The second ring went on two months after graduation. She had a degree in psychology, and our bond was sealed before God, family, friends, and the State of Tennessee. What a beautiful bride.

Were it not for our faith in God and help from family, the reaction may not have been sustainable. Free radicals need to learn discipline. Not everything we put into our marriage equation balanced. We had to learn what to take out and when to add more. Sometimes heat is produced when the wrong things are added. But, worse yet, sometimes the solution grows cold when a bad reagent is added.

Over time, the hot and cold reactions changed us; our highly charged opinions have been muted as they began to rub off on each other. It's a great thing when chemistry combines with psychology. Together there isn't any situation that we can't handle. Now we know each other's strengths and weaknesses, and how best to use them. We have a vast arsenal of problem-solving combinations at our disposal.

I'm writing this in my 20th year of a blessed marriage with Sue. Our two teenage children continue to grow under her warmth and guidance and possibly my analytic bent.

I loved you, Sue, from the moment I first saw you. To this day, when I look at you, I still see that teenage girl walking back and forth in front of my classroom. Back and forth. Back and forth.

FREDRICK G. DOLISLAGER is a Research Associate at the University of Tennessee, Knoxville, where he specializes in human health and environmental risk assessment.
http://web.utk.edu/~dolislag/

*Don't miss Fredrick's mom's love story in the anthology* Falling in Love with You: *"First Impressions...Aren't Always Stylish," by* Phyllis Porter Dolislager.

# An Ordinary Love Affair
## Francis and Frieda

\* \* \*

## GLORIA DOTY

Sparkling diamonds, luxurious furs, expensive candlelight dinners. In today's world, we equate these things with falling in love or being in love. My mother never owned a fur or a large diamond and was never treated to a candlelight dinner, and yet, she never doubted she was loved in a very special way.

Francis's family moved from Ohio to Indiana and rented a farm close to Frieda's family. The year was 1933; the country was in the throes of the Depression, and money for *fun* was nonexistent. Still, there were ways for young people to enjoy each other's company. They saw each other at church on Sunday mornings and at church youth meetings on Sunday evenings.

On one occasion, Frieda agreed to go to a barn dance with this tall, scholarly-looking young man. On the way to the dance his car had three flat tires. What a way to make an impression on a girl, but he must have made a good impression. They were married in August of 1935. They had $5 between them when they got married. The reception was at Frieda's parents' house and, in place of a fancy car, they arrived at the reception in a horse-drawn wagon.

After their marriage, they lived with Frieda's parents. Francis helped with the farm work and, in February of 1941, he began supplementing their income with a job in town. Every two weeks he earned $23.76 until April, when he received a two-cent an hour raise.

Their first daughter, Jeanette, was born in 1938; a second daughter, LaDonna, joined their family in 1942. By 1943, they had saved enough money for the downpayment on a house and seven acres. There was no indoor plumbing, and it was heated with a stove that sat in the living room, but it was *theirs*.

Then LaDonna became ill. Their little girl spent time in the hospital and endured many tests before she was diagnosed with leukemia. Despite all of the doctors' efforts and all the prayers for her earthly recovery, she died when she was just two-and-a-half years old. Her viewing was in the living room of the new house.

Many times, tragedies pull a marriage apart, but Frieda's and Francis's love for each other and their trust in God never wavered.

After Frieda's father died, her mother came to live with them. In 1946, after a miscarriage, another little girl, Gloria, was born to Francis and Frieda. It was ironic that Francis had only sisters when he was growing up, and now he still lived with a houseful of females.

Their daily lives consisted of very ordinary things. Frieda raised chickens and sold the eggs. She planted a large garden and canned countless jars of fruit, vegetables, and jam. She and her mother pieced and stitched a quilt every year.

In the summer of 1952, using only a shovel, Francis dug the deep holes needed for a septic tank. Now they could enjoy the luxury of an indoor bathroom. What a labor of love that was.

They attended church every Sunday, had devotions as a family every day, and always said their prayers and encouraged their children to do the same.

Although they were always conservative, there were some types of splurges. Every summer, they planned a motor trip to some area of the United States. Since Frieda didn't drive, it was solely Francis's responsibility to navigate the many miles of highway. Although they enjoyed these trips, they also used them to educate their children about different parts of the country, diverse groups of people, many national landmarks, and unbelievable scenery.

The other extravagance was connected to Francis's love of automobiles. He didn't want flashy or over-the-top models, just dependable, nice-looking cars. After paying off a loan for his first car, he ordered a new vehicle every two years. His trade-ins were in great demand, so a new one didn't carry a very huge price tag. Frieda would try to persuade him to keep the current car, but he would convince her to come to the dealership and choose the color she liked. She always accompanied him, a bit reluctantly, but enjoyed the new car when it arrived.

They lived within the traditional roles of husbands and wives of their generation. She took care of the domestic duties, and he took care of the financial things. She had her own money and could make her own purchases, but they always discussed large expenditures before making them. Although Francis was not a "surprise" kind of person, one Christmas, he did surprise Frieda with a new sewing machine.

And so they lived, day-to-day, year-to-year. They complemented each other in so many ways. Francis had been the valedictorian of his high school class, Frieda only finished eighth grade. She tended to be an extrovert, while Francis was more of an introvert. She truly enjoyed family reunions. He really never wanted to go; however he always *did* go because he knew how badly Frieda wanted to be there. They made compromises for each other. Francis didn't like tomato soup or grilled cheese. Frieda only made those two things when he would not be home for a meal. He wanted her to learn to drive, but when she resisted, he didn't push the issue. Frieda loved flowers and always had them planted, no matter where they lived. Francis really didn't care about flowers at all, but was always willing to till the beds and help plant them. He loved the West and considered moving to Arizona. She really did not want to leave all of her family. They compromised and moved 20 miles west instead of nearly 2,000.

Francis believed in being prepared. Statistics showed that the majority of men die younger than women. Francis wanted to move closer to Gloria's home so in the event he was the first to die, Frieda would be close to family. That was not to be.

Frieda died rather unexpectedly, in 1993, of congestive heart failure. For the first time in 58 years, Francis was alone. This was something he really had not prepared for. Every day, after lunch, for years, they would each take a nap in their recliners. After Frieda died, Francis claimed that he would wake up from his nap and see Frieda setting in her recliner. Perhaps he did. Perhaps God thought he needed a little more time to process the fact she was gone.

Francis slowly lost interest in the things he loved to do. He stopped reading, watching college basketball, and making wooden toys. He gave up the keys to his little red car, and he gave up enjoying life.

When he could no longer care for himself, he entered a nursing home. He developed Alzheimer's and, as the disease progressed, forgot nearly everything and everyone he knew. He would have occasional bursts of memory and then would say her name. "Frieda?" he would ask as though she were there.

They were reunited in December, 2002, when Francis also went to heaven.

Their marriage survived many things that tear couples apart: very little income in the first years, living with parents and then a parent living with them, the illness and death of a child, moving, and surgeries. Was their marriage perfect? No. Did they ever have disagreements? Of course. Did they go to bed angry with each other? Never.

This may seem like the most mundane, boring love story of all time.

However, perhaps this constant day-to-day respect, compromise, and interest in each other are the strongest threads in the "tie that binds" people together. They shared a faith in God and passed that legacy on to their children, by word and by example.

They were hard-working, ordinary people who shared an extraordinary love.

GLORIA DOTY, the mother of five and grandmother of 13, has had several occupations, but currently devotes my working time to her first loves: being a writer, author, and speaker. She writes two blogs: **www.gettingitright-occasionally.blogspot.com** and "Not Different Enough," published on **www.moms.fortwayne.com**. Both blogs are about the journey of 28 years with her autistic daughter.

# Child Bride

## * * *

## JUDY LEE GREEN

My mama, 10 years old, was playing paper dolls in a dry creek bed the first time she laid eyes on my daddy. Having cut her paper dolls from the Sears and Roebuck catalog hanging in the outhouse, she had carefully cut out a family—a mama and daddy and boys and girls of various ages and sizes.

For each of these dolls she had chosen and clipped numerous outfits, always taking the time to study the clothes in the children's section to see what she would wear if she were fortunate enough to wear mail-order clothes. She played alone, happy in a make-believe world with her paper playmates.

It was summertime. It was hot, and the creek was dry. My daddy was bored, riding his bike and showing off. He was 17 years old. Was he trying to aggravate or impress the little girl who was staying the summer with relatives?

Daddy had a reputation for doing stunts on his bicycle: riding on one wheel, standing on the seat while steering with his hands, and even riding his bicycle through the house. His mother often chased him out the back door with a broom or a mop, whatever she had in her hand, when his younger sister opened the screen door and he rode through the central hall.

Despite an awkward beginning, the fates of these two young people were forever sealed. Four years later, after finishing the eighth grade, my mama was married to my daddy in the middle of the night by a barefoot preacher who got out of bed and put his pants on but never bothered with his shoes.

His wife, her hair in curlers, put a robe over her nightgown, sat down in a rocker and crocheted while she moaned and cried throughout the ceremony, "You'll be sorry, child. Oh, child, you'll be sorry." These words are recorded in the family Bible.

After the ceremony the preacher's wife addressed my granddaddy. "Omer Bingham," she said, "you ought to be buggy-whipped, letting that baby get married."

My granddaddy bought my mama a toothbrush to celebrate the fact that she was being married and leaving home. She had never had a store-bought toothbrush. Like others in the family, she had previously brushed her teeth with a frayed sweet gum twig.

Mama put everything she owned in a brown paper bag, which was called a poke, and then it was nowhere near full. Other than her toothbrush and the clothes she wore, she had a faded work dress and a nightgown. Her underwear was made from flour sacks and feed bags.

"How would you like it if your underwear had the word *Purina* across the rear end and the head of a chicken on it?" she asked.

"And no matter how many times it was washed, no matter how hot the water boiling in the wash pot, or how strong the lye soap, neither the words Purina Chicken Feed nor the chicken itself disappeared," she told us. "Those drawers never even faded."

Though my mama was raised in the country, she had no idea what to expect on her wedding night. She went to bed with her clothes on and pulled the quilt up tight around her neck. When my daddy began trying to remove her clothes, one piece at a time, a wrestling match ensued. Daddy must have won that and several other wrestling matches, though, because my mama gave birth to five little babies in the next seven years, all by the time she was 21 years old.

Mama had a sweet tooth. She loved candy, anything with sugar in it, and she loved Coca-Cola. All Daddy had to do to have his way with her was to bring home a five-cent Hershey bar. Mama soon learned when this happened, however, that he had something other than dessert on his mind, something else entirely.

We five kids were stairsteps, just months apart, three boys and two girls. Mama loved us and loved sugar so much that she wanted us to love it too. She gave us Coke in our baby bottles and fed us sugar sandwiches. Almost daily she baked a cake or made a pie as a special treat. With seven of us in the family, it did not last more than a day. We had dessert for every meal. Mama became a wonderful cook, but even with fried chicken, fresh-dug potatoes, greens and pinto beans, creamed-style corn cut off the cob, and other tasty produce from Granddaddy's garden, Mama always ate her dessert first.

My mama and daddy were raised during the Depression. Times were hard. She was the daughter of a Georgia sharecropper, and he was the son of a Tennessee bootlegger who built houses when times were good. Times were bad, though, and when there was not enough demand for his building skills, my grandfather was forced to make a little whiskey to make ends meet and feed his family of 10.

Daddy had 21 dollars to his name when he and Mama married. He owned nothing more. He paid the preacher two dollars to perform the ceremony. Daddy, like his daddy and his brothers, was a carpenter. He was taken out of school in the fifth grade to work and help support the family.

When he and Mama married, my daddy was making 25 cents an hour building houses. He did not have a car. They walked most places they went or else hitched a ride with my Uncle Bo, daddy's brother, who owned a '34 Ford with a rumble seat.

After spending their first few nights of married life with Daddy's family, my parents rented a tiny two-room house with peeling paint and cold running water and a bare light bulb hanging down from the ceiling in each room. Neither of them had ever known such luxury.

Times were hard, but the economy following World War II was good, and my parents survived. "Use it up, wear it out, make it do, do without" was the adage by which they raised us kids in the late '40s and the 1950s.

Daddy bought a used 1947 Plymouth. It was black. There was no other color. He bought Mama a radio and then an ice box and a wringer washing machine. With his own hands he built us a small two-bedroom house on a steep 100-dollar lot covered in rock and scrub pines.

My parents never really had any hobbies or interests, other than each other. They were happy just to sit on the porch at night or walk hand-in-hand around the block. Mama loved the radio and sang along with Kitty Wells, Hank Williams, and other country music greats as she cooked, did the laundry, ironed the clothes, and cared for us kids throughout the day. After a television set was purchased, they had a Saturday night date to watch *Gunsmoke* with a bowl of popcorn.

Mama never wanted a bigger house, a nicer car, expensive vacations, fancy clothes, or jewelry. Neither of my parents ever had a wedding ring. She told me more than once, "If all your daddy could afford was a tent, I'd live in a tent."

Until the day he died, my daddy wanted nothing but to please my mama. They were married 46 years when he passed away from cancer. *Part of me died that morning,* Mama wrote of the day Daddy died. *We were married 46 years, three months, and five days. He was my husband, my lover, my friend.*

Theirs was a love story. Neither of them ever had a date with anyone else. And, in fact, they never had a date with each other until after they were married.

Did they ever have a disagreement, a fuss, a difference of opinion, a misunderstanding during their 46 years? Of course. But they did not quit.

Unlike couples today, they did not even threaten to quit.

My parents stood before God and promised to make a home together for better or for worse until death parted them, and they upheld their vow. They modeled a good marriage for us kids. They were a united front when we were growing up. We could never play them against each other.

They took us to church and taught us right from wrong. Mama seated us kids on the sofa at night, squeezed herself in the middle, and read us Bible stories. We learned from them by the way they lived their lives.

What do I know from growing up in a home with two loving parents who were committed to each other?

I know there was never anyone else for either of them.

I know they always called each other, "Baby."

I know that the little things in life are really the big things.

And I know that no matter what the preacher's wife predicted, my mama was never sorry.


JUDY LEE GREEN is an award-winning writer and speaker whose spirit and roots reach deep into the Appalachian Mountains. Tennessee-bred and cornbread-fed, she has been published hundreds of times and received dozens of awards for her work. Her colorful Southern family is the source for much of her inspiration. She lives in Murfreesboro, Tennessee.

# To Billie, I Love You, Lum

* * *

## KAY HARVIN

Billie and Lum knew each other as kids, growing up in a small town in Florida in the 1920s and '30s. Both families were honest, but poor, as were many families in that place and time. Both kids went by nicknames: Mary Lillian was Billie, and Woodrow was called "Boy" until he was 12 years old. In high school, Boy earned another nickname, "Lum," named after the cartoon characters, Lum & Abner.

Billie and Lum were well-liked in school and in the community: she, for her sweet disposition and pretty smile; Lum, for his sense of humor, intelligence, and good looks. They were the perfect couple and very much in love. He graduated from high school in 1937 and she in 1939. The whole town knew that one day they would marry.

Neither family had the money for a formal wedding, so Billie and Lum eloped. They drove to a neighboring county and were married by a Justice of the Peace on August 1, 1940. Not wanting to upset their parents, the newlyweds hid the marriage certificate in the glove box of the car. They often said to each other that they were just waiting for the right moment to reveal their secret. But, before they could, Billie's sister found the certificate and became the "town crier." Neither family was surprised or even upset, and wished them well.

Lum had mustered in the county's National Guard in 1940 as a way to supplement their income. His was a cavalry unit, activated in 1941 when the United States entered World War II. The cavalry unit was reorganized as artillery. Lum was shipped overseas to fight in the European Theatre. Two families and an entire community prayed for his safe return. They also prayed for the other men who were serving their country in war.

Lum was sent to North Africa, then Sicily, and then marched "up the boot" of Italy. He was also a paratrooper and made 22 successful jumps. Lum was wounded in combat in Italy and had to stay in a hospital there for eight months. He was struck by shrapnel on his back, shoulders, and in the face. He lost 70 percent of the vision in his right eye. But he had his life. Prayers were answered.

The brave soldier asked the medics to collect and save the bits of metal extracted from his body. As he slowly recovered from his wounds, Lum melted the metal shards and scraps and fashioned a heart-shaped piece of jewelry. The heart was large enough to dangle from a chain, to make a necklace. Engraved on the heart: *To Billie, I Love You, Lum.*

Lum kept the metal heart in his pocket during the rest of the tour, until he could give it to Billie in person. This he did in 1945. He had survived the war. They started a family and had a baby girl (the author of this story) in 1947 and another girl in 1950. They were a happy family.

For several years, everything went well. Lum retired from the U.S. Army and planned on attending the university to complete his education, which the war had interrupted. He frequently commented that, with the girls raised and his education completed, he and Billie could travel and enjoy life. Such was not to be the case.

Billie was diagnosed with breast cancer in late 1963. Family, friends, and the close-knit community prayed and prayed for her recovery. Even with surgery and chemotherapy, she succumbed to the disease in early 1964 at the age of 43. People questioned why a benevolent God would allow Billie to die. She was so kind to everyone and was still needed by her two teenage daughters. She and Lum had been through so much together: the war, raising a family, and working hard to become financially successful. The "good life" was about to start for them. Lum has just received the master's degree. At least, Billie lived to see that, but why did she have to die?

Some say "the good die young." That isn't much comfort to the survivors. The young family struggled in the months after Billie's death. Confused and "without a rudder," Lum and his daughters grew apart. They were still a family, but the one who held them all together was gone. The sisters became estranged, each coping the best they could. There was work for Lum, and the two girls had school to keep them occupied, but life wasn't the same.

The girls married and had children of their own. Lum went back to the university to earn his doctorate degree. The three were involved in daily tasks, raising a family, working, and furthering their educations. One daughter became a teacher and the other earned a degree in computer programming. It was as if Billie had been forgotten. Life still wasn't the same, that is, until Billie's influence was felt again.

After she had been gone for many years, her presence was keenly felt again by Lum and his daughters. One would think that time would dull the memories and weaken the impact she held over those remaining, but not in this case. Billie's gentle nature and kind spirit grew stronger in the later memories of her children and Lum. Maybe the "hiatus" was due to busy lives, or, perhaps, that was the way in which the family grieved: denial and keeping busy, at first, then strength through acceptance, many years later.

Maybe the memories of her were just dormant, waiting to be revived at a later date. The memories surfaced when they were needed the most. I believe that God works at His own speed, in His own way. He let Lum and the girls finally make their peace with what happened so many years ago. Feeling lost and angry gave way to understanding and acceptance. Closer to each other. And closer to God.


KAY HARVIN is a native Floridian who, as an Army brat, has lived abroad. A retired teacher, Kay has written for years. She holds three degrees and enjoys reading, writing, and attending writers' groups. Her love of history and animals inspired her first book, *Amazing True Dog Tales, From A to Z.*
   **amazingtruedogtalesfromatoz.vpweb.com**

# Almost Single Until the Rapture

### * * *

## LILIAN P. HOSFELD

Everyone in my inner circle and family asked me, "Lilian, do you have any desire to marry? Are you ready to be single until the Rapture?"

With brewing resentment covered by a smile I answered, "I can live as a single and serve the Lord Jesus until I die."

At 13 I committed my life to a Christian guy next door. We attended the same high school and church. Our daily interaction blossomed into a special friendship that became a romantic relationship. As Dad and Mom reminded me, "Lilian, you are too young to commit yourself."

My immature, self-centered reply was, "I am a 'one-man woman.'"

Mom and Dad laughed but did not realize that I was serious.

After I graduated from college ahead of my sweetheart, my job assignment moved me to another district so we visited less often. I met some bachelors who were interested in me, but my stubborn nature always kicked in. I decided not to entertain anyone because I had only one love of my life.

One day before Christmas, while I was on vacation, this special lover proposed to marry me. He said, "Lilian, our relationship has been going on for 13 years, and we need to start our own family now."

My immediate reply was, "Can you please wait until my younger sister graduates from college? Besides, it will hard for us to start our own family and at the same time support her. Would you please wait at least three years?"

"Sorry, I cannot wait any longer."

"Why? You waited this long, and now you cannot wait any longer?"

I expected his pain from my reply to be temporary. The following year I received the shocking news that the only love of my life was getting married. I skipped work and cried with friends. Hidden in my sweet image of a child of God was a festering wound that kept on growing. I was spiritually and emotionally devastated.

I went to Manila, Philippines, for a job-related conference and to see my former lover to verify the news. After hearing the heart-shattering truth from him, I felt like heaven and earth had swallowed me. I walked to the bus station with an empty head and a heart in denial. I cried, asking the Lord, "Is it my fault that we are so poor that I need to help my siblings? Where did I go wrong?"

Ten years later a praying mother and father who did not give up changed the course of my life. One day when I was in my late 30s, my mother called me. In a worried low tone she said, "Lillian, your dad and I are praying for you to meet a guy who will support your commitment to the Lord's ministry."

"Mother, I appreciate your prayer, but most of the men who show interest in me are either too old or too young. Besides, I feel no attraction to any of them."

My best friend Sasheen met her spouse through a dating catalog. She picked a guy for me from the same catalog. I was hesitant, thinking that getting married through a dating catalog would not work for me.

Sasheen drafted an introductory letter about me for this potential lover. She urged me, "Rewrite the note about yourself and watch if he will respond. There is no harm in trying."

Six months later Sasheen sent a letter to me, checking whether I had sent the note to the guy that she had chosen for me.

Before Christmas 1998 I prayed, "Lord, this looks impossible, but I will send a letter to a complete stranger. Your will be done." I mailed it secretly to avoid embarrassment.

A few days before Valentine's Day a handwritten letter arrived by snail mail from the stranger. Letters continued once a month until June of the same year.

One night, after an outreach visitation, a strong knock on the door of my boarding house startled me. "Lilian, you have an overseas call."

"Did you tell the person to call back because I was in the bathroom?"

"I did but he said, 'Please call Lilian because it is very important.'"

"Hello, this is Hal. I had planned to visit you in July, but now I would like to see you in September during the week of Founder's Day at Cebu Bible Seminary."

That day in September Hal showed compassion to a deranged lady at a Pizza Hut. His listening ears and respect for the culture of the Philippines caught my attention. His openness to serve, love, and support the Lord's work moved me.

After two weeks of dating, something special blossomed in my heart.

Early one morning I prayed, "If he'll propose, I will accept. But it is up to you, Lord."

The same day as we were shopping Hal told me, "Getting married is like jumping with a parachute. Disaster happens when the chute does not open." He smiled and led me to the jewelry store. "Would you like to pick a wedding ring?" I entered the shop and picked a plain gold ring, then was puzzled by his counteroffer, "What about a fancy-looking gold ring?" He bought that expensive wedding ring for me.

I felt like my feet did not touch the ground. I was floating on Cloud 9. My heart was beating as fast as a race horse's. I discovered at that point I was emotionally attached to him.

Yet I feared the future. I had responsibilities at the seminary and could not leave until a replacement was found. What if my parents disapproved of him? Then we cannot get married even if he bought me a wedding ring.

When I approached the president of the seminary he required us to be at a board of trustees meeting to present our decision to get married.

"What if you two wait for another year because it's hard to release Lilian without a replacement? Come back next year to marry her," the chairman of the board said.

"We cannot wait for another year, because we already middle aged."

Everybody left the meeting in silence. They took Hal to a place where he could get a taxi to the hotel.

I went to the boarding house, not knowing what would happen next.

Later we agreed that I would stay at the seminary until they found my replacement.

The following month a missionary couple from Australia came to the seminary and decided to stay. I was off the hook with God's help.

I bought my own ticket to see my parents. That way I would not owe them anything if they would not allow me to marry Hal.

Hal's two-week planned visit extended to almost a month. As part of our culture, we visited my parents to seek their approval for our marriage. They agreed and blessed our relationship.

We were engaged before Hal left the Philippines. I followed him to Utah. We were married on July 8, 2000 in Missoula, Montana, his home state.


LILIAN P. HOSFELD has been an Intercessor since 1987. She teaches a multicultural group Bible study and loves to prayer walk with her hubby's buddies: Indigo (Rottweiler), Toby (Chihuahua), and Xander (Doberman Pinscher).

**www.lilianhosfeld.com**

# Hunting for Love and Dinner

### * * *

## MARCIA HORNOK

"Why don't you come hunting with me these last three days of the season?" my husband said.

"Is Elk Fever making you that delusional? You know I don't enjoy hunting trips."

But Ken knows how to tempt me. "While I hunt, you can sit in the tent trailer and read all day or work on your book—think of the solitude." I couldn't believe he was encouraging me to write, when he usually thinks it takes too much of my time.

I began packing his food: homemade sweet rolls and muffins, steaks and burgers, sandwich meat and cheese. To me, the redeeming thing about hunting is breaking to eat. As I began a batch of brownies, my resistance weakened: *He shouldn't hunt alone—what if he gets hurt? We would have some time together. Shouldn't I try harder to love what he loves?*

I went to the garage where he was checking his gear. Crossing my arms in a protective gesture I said, "If I go along, would we stay only two nights? That's the max I can stand without washing my hair."

"I guarantee it."

"Will you take enough toilet tissue along? Last time we ran out."

"It's already packed."

"Okay then, I guess I'll go."

"Great! Do we have an extra sleeping bag?"

"Why?"

"It gets a little chilly at night. We'll buy one."

I learned long ago, no expense is extravagant when it comes to THE HUNT.

After loading the van and buying more *necessary* gear, we drove one hour on freeway and one hour on the equivalent of earthquake damage to get to Ken's spot. He hunted until dark while I tidied the tent trailer. The toilet tissue supply looked dauntingly small.

After a hearty dinner, we huddled around the butane heater and read until our hands numbed, then hunkered into sleeping bags and turned off the lanterns. In the dark, I set my glasses on the counter but missed and heard them clatter to the floor. *I'll find them in the morning.*

## The Morning Hunt

Up at 5:00, Ken lit the lantern and made coffee.

I roused and told him, "I can't find my glasses."

Neither could he. We took up mattresses, peered down every crevice with a flashlight. Finally I said, "You're going to miss sunrise; you'd better go. I'll find them."

"No," he said, "You can't see without them, so how would you find them?"

*Is he sacrificing prime hunting time for me?*

Eventually he spotted them. Somehow they had bounced sideways into a lower cupboard, chipping one lens.

After he left, I recocooned myself in my two sleeping bags and threw his on top for good measure. I didn't emerge until the sun did. Ken was right about solitude. My uninterrupted morning yielded rough drafts for two chapters of my book.

He returned elkless at noon. We lunched and napped. I decided to venture out with him for the afternoon hunt. Seeing my role as Comfort Station, I fortified our backpacks with snacks, water, extra clothes, a novel, and a dwindling roll of toilet tissue.

Recalling previous expeditions with me, Ken made me wear three layers of everything so I wouldn't be cold. He handed me an orange vest and ski cap. "Wear this hat to keep your head warm."

I recoiled. "I'll look terrible in that."

"No one will see you."

I pulled the cap on and we set off.

## The Endurance Hunt

Now I don't know why a hunter cannot stay near camp, hide behind a pine tree, and harvest the animal. Noooo, first we had to conquer the mountain.

"It's a little steep here, but it gets easier," Ken assured me.

"Where are the ropes and pitons?" I asked his back as he bounded upward.

Every 10 steps I had to rest. Ken waited for me at the top.

"You look funny in that hat," he said. "Now we go around this ridge. Try to walk quieter. Can you pant with your mouth closed?"

Sweating from exertion, I shed my outer coat. He carried it for me and we pressed on.

Suddenly he stopped and whispered, "Over there I got my first elk. I remember it as plain as day. It's kind of like your wedding night—you never forget."

"Good. Let's hunt there."

"No, we have to go a little farther; it's all downhill."

*NOW it's downhill. What about going back?*

Down the mountain, through the aspens, I pondered how killing a wild animal compared with our wedding night.

"This is where my brother gets his elk every year," my tour guide reported.

"Good. Can we sit here?"

"No. Too much human scent. The elk can smell everything 100 yards away. But you can go to the bathroom now."

"I don't have to go."

"Well, I don't want any human smells in the area where I will hunt, so try to go."

I took the last-chance rest stop on that interstate and used up the remaining toilet tissue.

We continued hiking across a meadow. He pointed to a dead tree, "Remember sitting there in '98 when you saw that herd come running through?"

"Sorry. I can remember our first kiss by the reservoir 33 years ago and how the moon reflected on the water, but I can't say I've ever been here before."

"Surely you remember—we had two feet of snow that year."

*Big mistake! If I hadn't successfully repressed that, I wouldn't be here.*

We trudged on. To divert my attention from the effort of hiking, I thought about that first kiss. Ken had said, "I love you," and I had declared the same. It was our first and only experience of being in love, and I've never regretted that Ken has been the only man to kiss me. I haven't missed out on anything. Instead, we've fallen in love repeatedly over the roller-coaster years that make up a marriage.

Now, here we were supporting each other's hobbies and being together through adventure and adversity.

102

Finally after what seemed like another hour, and five more hunting landmarks pointed out, Ken whispered, "We have to be quiet now. The elk can hear everything 200 yards away."

I wondered how someone had studied elk sensory skills so precisely. Nevertheless, I tried to walk on dry leaves without swishing and keep my water bottle from sloshing.

## The Elk Hunt

At last we arrived at the Sacred Hunting Ground and sat down in THE SPOT. I ate dried fruit and granola bars and drank most of my water. Ken ate the same plus trail mix and bagels. *I was right about food being the best part.*

Ken hunted. I read, dutifully looking around for elk every time I wiggled a finger out of my wool mitten to turn a page.

Two hundred pages later, the sun set. So did my pelvic joints. Ken pried me up, and helped uncrimp my back. "Now we'll move to a pond. The elk drink there after sunset."

*For someone who knows so much about elk...* but I didn't say it aloud.

At the pond we sat—I mean hunted—for 30 minutes. Evidently the elk weren't thirsty. Our water, however, was gone. I had to go to the bathroom but didn't want to violate the area. My hands were too cold to hold the novel. My scalp itched.

Finally Ken admitted we should head back before it got too dark. We hiked over the meadow, up the draw, through the aspens, around the ridge. In my head I crafted a book chapter about suffering.

Ken stopped as often as I needed, but soon the moon was high overhead. At least now I could pant openly. I tripped once and my glasses went flying. We felt around the leaves until we found them, bent frames and all.

We reached the last summit and began descending to camp. Ken took my hand to steady me, but romance was in the gesture.

"I'm sorry you didn't see any elk," I said.

"That's okay. I'm glad you came along. You don't regret it, do you?"

I didn't hesitate. "No, the important thing is we're together. We need to encourage each other's pursuits like this more often."

"Yes, I thought you'd be my lucky charm," he replied, putting his arm around me. "Maybe next time."

"Could we have a few ground rules next time?"

"Like what?"

"Like how far from camp we hike, how long we sit in the cold, and how much toilet tissue we stock. There's none for tomorrow, and frankly, I'm going to use pages from the Hunting Proclamation."

"I'll bring more next time," he promised. "Now, what's for dinner?"

MARCIA HORNOK writes from Salt Lake City, where Ken pastors Midvalley Bible Church and hunts in the Wasatch Range. Marcia admits that the best thing about hunting is elk steaks, but that takes cooperation on the part of the huntee, which never seems to happen when she accompanies her husband. She is Managing Editor of *CHERA Fellowship* magazine for widowed persons and the *Salt Lake Biblical Truths Examiner* at **www.examiner.com/user-marcia-hornok.**

**http://christiangals.blogspot.com/**

# Meant To Be
## A Love Story of 70 Years

\* \* \*

### MARY DODGE ALLEN

My Uncle Gordon, who flew a B-17 bomber during WWII, now guides my Aunt Dorie's wheelchair through their assisted living facility. At the usual time for their coffee break, he parks her chair next to the café table at precisely the right angle for her to reach her place setting with her only good hand. As soon as he sits down, Gordon turns her coffee cup upright and slides her plate closer to her. "How is that?"

They gaze at each other for a moment, and I see, reflected in their eyes, the vibrant love that has endured the stressful separation of a world war, several cross-country moves, the loss of their only son to cancer, and now the struggles of aging.

"That's fine." Dorie nods. Her stroke has left her with partial paralysis, but her mind is still sharp. Gordon often looks to her for assistance whenever his short-term memory fails him. But his memories of the old days are remarkably clear.

In response to my question, he describes how they met, in 1940. "It was the first day of bookkeeping class at Duluth Business College." He describes how his attention was immediately captured by the stunningly attractive brunette sitting at one of the desks. "I liked it that she wasn't wearing heavy makeup, like so many of the girls did back then. She had a natural look." He pauses. "As soon as I saw her, I knew she was the one."

"Didn't I have any say in the matter?" Dorie laughs. "What if I hadn't said yes?"

He shakes his head, as if he knew it was simply meant to be.

The classroom was set up with benches for two, and wide desks to share. "I made sure I sat next to her," he says.

"He never let anyone else sit next to me." Dorie's deep blue eyes brighten with this memory. Her face, now framed with wavy gray hair, is still attractive without a hint of makeup.

"Well, someone had to help you with your bookkeeping," he says, teasing her.

"And someone had to help you with your typing." Dorie smiles.

"That's right. I was a terrible typist."

The waitress arrives with their order—coffee all around and an oatmeal cookie to share. Gordon pours exactly the right amount of cream in Dorie's coffee and stirs it for her. He offers me a portion of their cookie, which I decline. He then splits it in half and places the larger piece on Dorie's plate.

"Times were hard back in those days," Gordon says. "I earned the money I needed for business college by working for several months in the CCC camp." He describes the long days he spent working for the Civilian Conservation Corps planting row after row of trees in northern Minnesota, where heavy logging had deforested the area. "We lived in barracks, like the military, and we wore old wool uniforms that had been stored in mothballs since WWI. We got free room and board and were paid a dollar a day. The government sent 25 dollars to my bank account every month, and I got to keep five dollars for spending money."

I ask how long they dated. "All the rest of that school year," Gordon says. "I didn't have much money to spend, after paying for college. We'd go out to the movies—they cost less than a quarter back then. And when we went out to eat, we often shared a meal, didn't we?"

Dorie nods as she reaches for the halved cookie on her plate. "I didn't care what we did, as long as we were together."

"We spent a lot of evenings at her folks' house, listening to radio programs." Gordon suddenly grins as he glances at Dorie. "I remember a few times I stayed so late, I had to run to catch the last bus back home."

They were married in 1941, in a simple ceremony, and they lived with Dorie's parents at first, to save money. She continued to work as a clerk in her father's small grocery store. "Jobs were scarce," Gordon says, "but I was lucky. I found a job at the Steel Plant."

When they finally saved up enough, they rented their first furnished apartment in Duluth.

"We didn't stay there long," Dorie says. "It had bedbugs."

"The landlady accused us of bringing them in." Gordon's voice still carries the sting of indignation.

Dorie smiles. "Do you remember your nickname for her?"

He stops for a moment and struggles. Then his face breaks into a sheepish smile. "Mrs. Weakleg."

"Her name was Armstrong," Dorie explains, giggling.

106

"As soon as we could, we found a cleaner apartment in West Duluth," Gordon says.

A few months after Pearl Harbor, he enlisted in the Army Air Corps. "I knew I would be drafted," he says, "and if I had to serve, I wanted to be a pilot. I remember, as a boy, looking up whenever a plane flew overhead and wishing I was inside it, looking down."

Gordon trained as a copilot on a B-17 Flying Fortress bomber, and was stationed in England in 1944. He flew 35 missions to Germany and beat the odds by surviving the brutal flak and antiaircraft fire that downed so many planes. Only about one-third of all B-17 crewmembers survived the required 35 missions.

"He sent me a telegram after every mission," Dorie says.

"There were pre-made telegram forms available on the base," he says. "They had a list of one-line messages, and you checked the box next to the one you wanted to send."

"I sure looked forward to those telegrams, and letters," Dorie says. She shifts her gaze to Gordon. "I prayed for you every day, but I never really considered the possibility that you wouldn't come back. You promised me you'd come home, and I believed you."

Gordon smiles. "We had plenty of prayers lifting up our crew. Ralph, our pilot, had a father who was a minister. I'm sure his father had the whole congregation praying for us." His expression saddens. "Ralph was a great guy. He became a minister, too, after the war." He tells me that Ralph passed away three years ago. My uncle, at 92, is now the last living member of his B-17 crew.

Gordon rises slowly from his chair, using his cane for support. His tall frame is only slightly stooped with age and arthritis, and his thick silver hair is neatly combed back from his chiseled face. He hooks his cane onto the back of Dorie's wheelchair, unlocks the wheels and then guides her away from the table. I walk beside them down the wide hallway leading to the nursing center, and I watch as they greet their friends. Gordon, always a tease, has a witty, playful comment for everyone. A few people jokingly ask Dorie how she has been able to put up with him all these years.

"Patience," she says.

A pink envelope rests on top of the colorful afghan draped over my aunt's lap. Inside is a card they recently received from their daughter-in-law, with photos of their two grandsons, who are both in college. Earlier, while we were in the café, they showed me these photos and spoke with pride about how well their grandsons are doing. Left unspoken was how proud their son would have been of them, too.

Gordon will add these photos to the others posted on the bulletin board next to Dorie's bed. Since her stroke, she has had to reside in the nursing center wing of the facility, while he remains in their assisted living apartment. They both hate living apart, but Gordon faithfully visits her at least three times a day.

We reach the nursing center, and he parks her wheelchair in the activities room. It is time for Dorie's physical therapy and medication. He sets the brakes and then leans down, with difficulty, to give her a kiss. "Love you, Hon." He reaches for her good hand and gently holds it.

Dorie looks up at him. "Love you, too."

"I'll be back, later."

She nods, believing.


MARY DODGE ALLEN, a former teacher/counselor/social worker and volunteer at her local police department. She won the Word Weavers/Christian Writer's Guild Writing Contest in 2008, has published nonfiction articles in college, community, and city newspapers, such as the *Orlando Sentinel,* and newsletters for The Nature Conservancy and the Dallas Community College System. She's married, the mom of one adult son, and is currently writing an inspirational romance set in Florida.

**marydodgeallen.com**

# Love Blossoms

## * * *

## MELISSA DAVIES

As a young girl I often entertained ideas of being rescued by a prince on a mighty white steed. I would dream of my own family, with visions of a homemade pie cooling in the windowsill, children playing in the backyard, and the sweet embrace of my husband home from a hard day of work. Little did I know that, one day at a time, this hope of my childhood became a reality.

It was my senior year of high school and thoughts of a husband were distant to me as I considered my pursuit of college and the importance of a career. Honestly, I thought it was "too late" to have a high school sweetheart. In the first class of fall semester, though, I noticed a certain boy. He was nicely dressed and kind. However, he obviously kept looking at my school work, so I decided he had to be a liar and a cheat.

As weeks went by, I built up the nerve to confront him about my assumptions. But when I began to express just what I thought about him, he interrupted me and started questioning my character! As the words settled, he explained he was only looking at my school work to learn my name. I believed him willingly and blushed. It turned out he was not only kind and handsome but also really smart. We had more in common than anyone either of us met in our life. I enjoyed being with him.

I knew from past turmoil I should guard my heart, so I tried. The thoughts of attending college out of state helped get my mind refocused on my career. There was only one college I had longed to attend. But when I received the letter of acceptance, it included the condition of a two-year wait. My heart paused. I did not want to wait two years. I started to consider other options. This boy who was a valued friend requested to court me for marriage. Weighing my childhood dreams of being a wife and mother with the importance placed on a career now delayed, I found peace and delight in those thoughts of a little happy home. After two or three weeks I accepted. We made it official and began our rollercoaster of a courtship.

Our high school Ecology class took a trip to a wild life refuge. With our peers and chaperones we all boarded the buses with excitement. The ride was a blur with the anticipation of the beauty we would behold. Our arrival was timely. I searched the faces to find my beau. To my delight, our eyes met. I sheepishly strolled through the crowd until our shadows touched. My heart was jittery in his presence. He is tall and strapping. His eyes are as dark as the Atlantic and his thoughts just as deep. He looks at me with adoration and love. My mind wondered at our pursuit of life and our future together.

We quietly waited, attempting to read and confirm the other's desires. Our instructor hastened our group aboard a small barge. This day was better than any dream. The cool water splashed against the shore—the trees all stood at attention declaring the glory of their design, vibrant with life—some with blossoms of soft pink and creamy white. A slight breeze carried the melody of birds in joyful praise. In my mind the fish could have been swimming to the same beat of harmony and love.

Some commotion on board revealed a crane balancing itself on a rock edge. As the cameras flashed the hustle of activity soon gave way to a hush. We all gazed at a mighty eagle circling a towering tree and then settling on its nest. What a sight! My eyes had never beheld such a creature content in its own habitat with a feeling of purpose.

My focus shifted to my beau in wonder if he witnessed this moment. Without a word spoken his expression was mutual awe. As I examined his countenance, I knew my heart was in love with him. (This moment in time engraved itself within my mind and is reflected in my heart every time I see the calm waves of a water's edge.) We shared a picnic lunch by the observatory and our hearts were knit together with love. That day I realized this man, Eric, was who I desired to pledge my love and adoration to for life.

The months rolled into years. I was beginning to be a bit weary of the thoughts of possible marriage since he continually delayed his proposal to me. I was so downhearted that I reluctantly decided to call the whole thing off. I assumed it would be too much unneeded care and stress.

While standing in my gravel driveway, with a nervous but firm explanation of our necessary separation, he grabbed a ring from the glove box of his jeep and then dropped on one knee. He said there will be troubles and cares, but if we were together we would have each other to get through them. He gave a convincing speech, I was so astonished and caught up in the moment, I missed his proposal!

I realized he must have asked me the question because he stopped talking and was staring at me with this beautiful ring revealed from its gray box.

Needing to be sure, I asked him to repeat what he just said.

The scene seemed crazy, wrought with conflicting emotion. I nervously laughed and pushed him, telling him he was not being serious. He was serious, and he repeated his proposal. Fully persuaded, I joyfully accepted.

So our courtship blossomed into an engagement, and our engagement to marriage. I still remember the hectic dressing rooms and having to manage my bridesmaids' diverse personalities, the pictures that never got taken, and my bouquet that I forgot all about until right before I was to walk the aisle. Though everything did not go as beautifully as I anticipated; I was more than happy. Somewhere down the aisle my mind stopped thinking about who was present and where the photographer would go next. I saw my prince, I heard his oath of endearment, and we exchanged those precious vows. As the ending of the ceremony drew near, the maid-of-honor handed me my bouquet. When the minister pronounced, "You may now seal this covenant with a kiss," to keep this moment as our own, I lifted my bouquet to shield our kiss from the sight of the audience. We were happier than ever before, ecstatic to finally belong to each other.

We enjoyed our reception and he carried me out to whisk me away to our honeymoon. We rode a ferry from the Carolinas to Ocracoke Island. We shared our first home there for a week. We enjoyed the view of a lighthouse from the back porch and dined on powdered doughnuts and milk under the stars. We relished each moment, knowing this was the beginning of our own special story. We returned home destined to preserve and nurture the hopes shared within each of us.

I would like to say things were perfect and we lived happily ever after but that would be a fairy tale. He was right: we have faced troubles. We have been caught at times in the cares of this life. At times the everyday life has taken its toll and we have found ourselves worn by the assault. We have, however, gone through all of it together, ready with support and encouragement for each other. Life has given our faith plenty of lessons on what it means to choose to love each other. We remember our pledge of love before many witnesses on that warm Saturday in April. We sincerely made the choice then to love each other for the rest of our lives, in sickness and in health, for richer and for poorer, for better and for worse, and we are keeping every word. Such loyalty and dedication breeds peace and strength within our little happy home.

We constantly are understanding aspects of love that we had not considered within its definition. When it comes to expressions of love, many in our society only portray a fraction of the true depth and blessedness that it contains. God is love, and he has given us this gift to have during our portion of life. Just as a rainbow stretches over the sky, revealing an array of majestic colors, likewise, love reveals the goodness in others. Love can hide a multitude of mistakes; it produces emotions and carries burdens. Love eases hardships and molds the individual into perfection. May we all cherish those we love and appreciate the value of the words "I love you."

MELISSA DAVIES is the author of three faith-based children's books and several gospel songs. She and her husband, Eric, met in 2003. After a year of friendship and two years of courtship, they married and currently have two children. They have been actively involved in ministry work since 2002. Eric and Melissa make their "little happy home" in middle Tennessee.

# Divine Intervention

*  *  *

## MIMI PEEL ROUGHTON

I wasn't raised in the Episcopal Church at all. In fact, I considered the Episcopalians in my eastern North Carolina hometown strange. That they genuflected, crossed themselves, and knelt seemed exotic.

At my church, we stayed put even for Communion—just tiny glasses of grape juice, not real wine like at the Episcopal Church, where everyone drank out of the same chalice—so devil-may-care.

As an adult, I yearned to sing again in a church choir. Living in Bellingham, Washington, one February day I drove into town planning to compare several churches of different denominations, then choose one. I walked around St. Paul's Episcopal while frigid wet air whipped in off Puget Sound. A stocky man in priest's collar and overcoat strode past. He gave me a stunning smile and spoke such a friendly greeting that it was decided: That was my new church.

My marriage wasn't good, and St. Paul's became the center of my life. The friendliness Father John showed me wasn't random. He had the remarkable ability of remembering the name of every person he met. He essentially preached one sermon every week—Love Thy Neighbor. I loved the welcoming people at St. Paul's.

I was captivated by the Church because, as a branch of England's Anglican tradition, the faith embraced beautiful ancient rituals as well as reason and personal discernment. I always felt lighter after a service, stronger for facing my life as a *de jure* married but *de facto* single mother and stepmother.

One Sunday morning, sun glowing through the stained-glass windows onto my hands as I knelt at the altar during Eucharist, I was certain I felt the Holy Spirit move through me. It was a moment of clarity, alertness, and a vague excitement about what the future held, although I couldn't begin to imagine what that was. Being an Episcopalian was still a huge part of my tattered identity when an excruciating divorce forced me to leave

Bellingham—and St. Paul's.

When Lily, my nine-year-old daughter, and I moved to Durham, North Carolina, I was emotionally broken, fearful about the future, but not, it turned out, unresilient.

An older woman—an Episcopalian, as it happened—invited me to lunch. When I told her I'd like to marry again, she said, "Pray for it. That's what *I* did, and it worked for me." I gave it a try, praying for "a wonderful husband."

One night Lily and I were at home when a group of Christmas carolers came to our door. Someone said, "Grab your coats and join us!" We ended up at a convivial after-party where I was invited to join the choir at St. Stephen's, the Episcopal church with striking modern architecture near our house.

So on a cold Wednesday night—January 6, 1999—I took Lily to the Epiphany service at St. Stephen's to check out what young people were doing in that parish.

Sitting close together in our pew, we struggled against church giggles at the antics of a particularly exuberant young teenager with curly black hair. We both noticed a distinguished-looking man sitting across the aisle in a dark overcoat, black hair brushed rather dashingly back from his swarthy but handsome face. His eyes, beneath arching eyebrows, caught mine more than once. "Mom, that man keeps looking over here. He reminds me of Lucifer. Is he wearing a black cape?" whispered Lily.

The man introduced himself to us at the post-service reception. His name was Lucien, not Lucifer. I told him my mother's name—Lucia--was essentially the same as his. His son was the kid who had made us laugh. He mentioned that his birthday was coming up the next month, on Valentine's Day.

"That was my father's birthday!" I said.

Over Epiphany cake containing little pieces of "treasure," Lucien and I discovered we'd both intended to speak to the choir director about joining the choir.

The following Sunday morning I arrived at St. Stephen's for choir and was told to go stand "there" on the bottom step of the risers, where everyone else was already assembled in choir robes. I was acutely aware that Lucien was directly behind me. Within moments he leaned down and whispered in my ear, "That's my son up there acolyting."

"I know," I whispered back.

Lucien later revealed that lame comment had been the best he could come up with on the spur of the moment. That he'd been looking for an excuse to get close enough to smell my hair, that when he did he was overcome by the fragrance of me. Our attraction was mutual and immediate.

I found out that Lucien was a cradle Episcopalian—his grandfather had been an Episcopal priest. Lucien was an architect, which seemed so glamorous. He didn't seem to mind that I worked as a lowly secretary to support Lily and myself. We courted at choir practices and other church events that followed Epiphany—the Fat Tuesday Pancake Supper and Ash Wednesday service. An Evensong service always followed choir practice; our favorite line in the litany implored God to "shield the joyous." Then we'd convene for an after-choir party in the kitchen. Afterwards, we'd walk slowly to our cars and linger.

By Easter Lucien and I had fallen deeply in love.

One wintry weekend I took Lucien down to my hometown to eat at the old oyster bar there, and we ran into my great-aunt on Main Street. Resembling Katherine Hepburn in a periwinkle blue headscarf that matched her eyes, this inimitably Southern Katherine anointed us: "Y'all look like you INVENTED love."

Lucien's and my relationship was passionate—and volatile—but neither of us even considered dating anyone else, and we never once broke up. Eventually—three-and-a-half years to the day after I arrived in Durham—he proposed, with Aretha Franklin's flawless version of "Say a Little Prayer for Me" playing in the background. We got married at St. Stephen's, of course.

This January, celebrating the anniversary of our first meeting, we returned to our church's Epiphany service. The hushed chapel felt cool, expectant, electrically charged. At the end, after the blessing but before anyone had left their pews, Lucien broke the respectful silence: "Folks, I want to say, Mimi and I met right here, thirteen years ago tonight."

Our life together has certainly not been perfect, but we remain soul mates of the highest order. I don't use that expression lightly. Lily always rolls her eyes when adults say they've found their soul mate, because her father claimed he'd found his in the woman he left me for—the one he left two years later. But I really don't know what else to call what Lucien and I have.

We still attend church together; I enjoy the music, fellowship, and the almost mystical way a Eucharist lightens my worries. But Lucien's off-the-cuff graces before meals, his speaking from his heart and addressing the concerns of that particular day, and his expression of gratitude for our chance to make a home together during our short time on earth, mean more to me now than any formal litany.

We still occasionally erupt into anger. Yet Lucien's the kind of husband who comes in the door at day's end play-bellowing, "Where's my wife? I love my wife!"

The way I've chosen to look at it, Divine Intervention led me to become an Episcopalian so I could meet the love of my life.

Epiphany, or Twelfth Night—much celebrated in the Anglican tradition—is the night the Magi brought gifts to the Christ child. I claim those wise men, in keeping with their generosity of spirit, gave me a gift, as well. In the service used on Epiphany, *The Book of Common Prayer* reads, "Be our light in the darkness, O Lord." If Jesus brought light to the world, then Epiphany 1999 brought light into the dark world of pain and loss where I'd been dwelling. I believe the Magi—or Jesus--brought me this man whose very name *means* light.

Lucien is, for me, *the brightest and best of the stars of the morning*. He is *as brilliant as a golden sunrise*. With him *I now hear the sound of music clear*. His is *the splendour which comes my way*. All that is the lovely language you hear at an Episcopal Epiphany service.

A brainy friend of mine believes real life is random—that it's not until you organize events into literature or art that meaning and connections arise. But I see powerful connections crisscrossing my life every day.

One thing I believe down to my molecules—from across the continent, from across the aisle, to beside me in bed every night until death do us part— *in my life there are no coincidences*.


**MIMI PEEL ROUGHTON** is a former journalist turned personal essayist. She lives in Durham, North Carolina, with her husband, Lucien. Between them, they have five children, all of whom have flown the nest.

# Bell Bottom Trousers

## * * *

## MONA ROTTINGHAUS

Chuck was disgusted.

"June, how could you do that to Jerry? He's my friend!"

"I'm marrying Bill and that's that, Chuck," June retorted. As far as she was concerned, the matter was settled and the conversation over.

Chuck pondered the situation. June, his younger sister, had just informed him of the letter she'd sent informing Jerry she was marrying someone else. Jerry, his closest friend, was overseas, in battle as a Chief Petty Officer in the Navy. *No man wants to receive that dreaded "Dear John" letter.* Chuck's heart sank. Somewhere in the South Pacific Jerry was on a ship getting a mail call that must have been a stab in his heart. *I wanted him for a brother-in-law.* Chuck sighed.

Gerald Henry Kies, known as Jerry to his wide circle of friends, was the eldest son of William and Anna Wester Kies. A handsome man in his naval uniform, he was one of the hardest workers Chuck knew. The eldest of nine children, he'd begun working at a young age for area farmers to help support his family. As a young teen he once challenged his employer for taking advantage of him. He was the kind of man Chuck wanted to keep in his life. A marriage to his sister would have ensured that. And now that dream was over. Chuck feared the same fate for their friendship.

Shortly after June disappointed him with her actions, Chuck watched his young sister-in-law interact with his children during the evening meal. Rita Ann Kremer, 17, had come to stay with them. Rita diced the potatoes and carrots for Mary, age one. His tiny daughter pinched a carrot between her chubby finger and thumb and attempted to take a bite. It promptly dropped on her bib. Rita giggled as she picked up the carrot. Mary dutifully opened her mouth and Rita popped it in for her. Chuck witnessed this exchange and a plan came to his mind.

"Rita, do you like to write letters?"

"Sure, why?"

"I have a navy buddy who could sure use a lift these days. Would you send him a letter? Send a photo of yourself, too, while you're at it." He chuckled. Rita was beautiful, high-spirited and full of laughter. *Just what Jerry needs to take his mind off that younger sister of mine,* he thought. *Perhaps I can still get Jerry as a brother-in-law, yet.*

"I can do that." Rita replied nonchalantly, but her heart skipped a beat. "Men in uniform are so handsome."

She thought carefully as she penned the words on the stationery. Her first draft ended crumbled in the wastebasket in the corner of her room. She began again. When she felt confident in what she'd written, she folded it carefully and placed it in the matching envelope. She tucked in her favorite photo. She was leaning on the front porch wearing pedal pushers and a smart blouse. In flowing penmanship she copied the address Chuck had given her earlier that day, attached the three cent stamp to the corner, and hurried to the mailbox to post the letter.

*How long will it take to get to him? Will he write back?* Rita wondered as she placed the letter in the box, lifted the red flag to signal the mailman of the outgoing mail, and returned to the house. It was time to start the evening meal for the Temeyer family.

A few weeks later Rita bounced up the lane. She had a reply from Jerry. She ripped open the envelope and skimmed the words on the page. She hummed the popular song "Bell Bottom Trousers" as she went about her chores.

The following Sunday morning, Rita attended Mass with Chuck while Tillie and the children stayed at home. Rita, always curious, looked at the congregation. A sailor sat next to William and Anna Kies. She found it hard to concentrate on the service; her mind and eye wandered continually to the dashing serviceman across the church. When the final hymn was sung, she made her way to the center aisle next to Jerry. Chuck fell in step behind them.

"Perhaps you could join us for coffee?" Jerry's mother, Anna, inquired.

"We'd love to come," Chuck replied as he patted Jerry on the back. "I want to catch up a bit with this guy."

It was settled. Chuck and Rita drove to the Kies family home. The family gathered around table as Anna poured cups of dark, black coffee for all. She carried a plateful of fresh cookies. "Have a cookie," she instructed everyone as she seated herself on the remaining chair.

Rita, nervous, looked at the cup of hot brew placed before her. She'd never tasted coffee. *No time like the present,* Rita thought as she picked up the cup. She blew gently across the top of the beverage as she'd watched her father do countless times and took a small sip. Quickly she set the cup on the saucer, her eyes darting around to see if anyone had noticed her obvious distaste. Rita breathed a sigh of relief.

Chuck and Jerry were deep in conversation. She noticed a bowl of sugar cubes a few inches from her cup. Carefully picking up the tongs, she placed one small cube in her coffee, stirred the liquid to dissolve the sugar, and made a second attempt to try the drink. She lowered her cup and her eyes as the hot bitterness slid down her throat.

A small pitcher of cream was beside the sugar bowl. Rita willed her hand to be steady as she reached for the ceramic container and added some to her cup. Along with the cream, she added two more cubes of sugar. Conversation continued around her as she tried the coffee again. *Still needs more*, she said to herself as she added more cream and sugar.

When Anna offered her a cookie, Rita hoped the sweetness of the dessert would enable her to finish her cup of coffee. She nibbled at the cookie and took tiny sips of coffee until her cup was empty. At one point she peeked over her cup at Jerry and met his eyes as he glanced at her. Barely a word was spoken by Rita, but the silence was filled by Jerry and Chuck.

Soon it was time to leave. Chuck and Rita thanked the Kies family for their hospitality and returned to the Temeyer home. As Chuck chatted about seeing his long-time friend, Rita thought about the short encounter. She wasn't sure what attracted her about Jerry. Was it his good looks, or his uniform? Later that afternoon Jerry called her.

Rita's heart raced as she listened. "Yes, I would love to go to a movie tonight. I will be ready," she said as she breathlessly hung up the phone. She dashed to her room and chose a fresh dress. She washed her face, pinched her cheeks to give them additional color, and applied a smear of lipstick. She fidgeted in the chair as she waited for Jerry to arrive.

Over the next two weeks the pair saw each other every day; going to movies, out to dinner, and falling in love beneath a harvest moon. Before he left to join his shipmates at sea, Jerry asked for Rita's hand in marriage and she whispered, "Yes."

The 18-month courtship was completed through letters, postcards, and photographs. Rita wrote each day to Jerry and met the mailman daily in hopes of a return letter from him. She read and re-read every letter, carrying them with her as she did her daily responsibilities.

In March 1945 the mailbox at Rita's home was empty. Agonizing weeks passed until Anna, Jerry's mother, phoned and read the telegram from the U.S. Navy:

The Navy department deeply regrets to inform you that your son, Gerald Henry Kies, chief gunner's mate, U.S.N., has been seriously wounded in action. Diagnosis: wounds multiple left arm and chest. When further details are received, they will be forwarded to you promptly. The Navy department joins you in the wish for your son's speedy recovery.—Vice Admiral Randall Jacobs

In July 1945, Jerry returned to duty aboard the battleship *U.S.S Nevada* after receiving the Purple Heart Award. Later that year, just before Christmas, Rita received a package in the mail that held her engagement ring.

On January 14, 1946 Jerry was discharged from the Navy. One month later, on Valentine's Day, Jerry and Rita were married. Jerry and Rita, my parents, lived on the same farm for over 40 years and raised 11 children.

October 15, 2002 Dad was diagnosed with cancer. A few short days passed and Dad was hospitalized. Our family surrounded them continually. On October 21, we all stepped out of the hospital room to give my parents some private time.

Mom wrapped her arms around him. "It's okay, Jerry. Go in peace." Rita's final kiss ushered him home.

MONA ROTTINGHAUS, the mother of four and grandmother to four, lives on a farm in Iowa with her husband. She has owned and operated Mona's Originals, an apparel decorating company, for 18 years. Other interests are sewing, writing, and upcycling items.

**monatheoriginal.blogspot.com**

# Dancing into Canada!

## * * *

## MONIKA DYCK-SCHNEIDER

My husband and I had celebrated our 40th wedding anniversary with family and friends when we were invited to a military luncheon. I sat next to the Padre, and during our conversation he asked me how Marv and I had met and my immediate response was: it was an accident. At least, it seemed that way at the time. But today I know it was divine providence that brought two lonely souls together.

I had been raised by my mother's parents and her only sister after World War II in Germany after I lost my parents when I was three days old. We lived in a small town close to a Canadian military base, and when I was in my teens, I became good friends with one family. When their tour of duty was over and they left, I thought I should travel to Canada some time if all people there were kind and generous. But my vacation time was limited, and life moved on.

One summer day, when I was 21, I spent the day with my elderly grandmother, driving her to visit her sister-in-law in the hospital. When we returned in late afternoon my aunt met me at the door and told me that David, the Canadian neighbour across the street, had come over to ask if I would join him, his wife, and their friend Marvin for the evening to dine and dance. He explained that they had really looked forward to this outing—their first one after the baby was born, and a sitter had been arranged. But then Marvin's date had cancelled. He would not have anyone to dance with as the restaurant where they had reservations was known as a great place for couples only. David had been at the door several times, hoping I'd be back in time and agree to go with them.

I was in no mood to go out on a date for a whole evening with someone I didn't know, and I was also tired. But my aunt said: "You should go with them. We are Christians, and they are strangers in our country. Now they have made all the arrangements for the evening, and they can't go without you."

Shortly after that, David again came to ask, and I could not say no. I was introduced to Marvin. He was tall, blond, blue-eyed, polite and quiet, and an amazing dancer.

On our way home he asked me if I would like to go to the nearby airport with him on the next weekend. He would be sky-diving there as he belonged to the club. That sounded very exciting to me. I'd often heard and watched the small planes from there fly over our community but to be invited by a sky diver, well, I couldn't pass that up.

In the evening Marv invited me to the officers' Mess on the Canadian base where we had dinner. I met the group of people who spent much of their free time together—15 single officers and 12 single female teachers who lived close by.

Up until then my life had been like black-and-white photos, the black representing the constant grieving of the many losses and the effects of war and the white our few celebrations mainly in church. Now I was experiencing life in colour: the group at the officers' Mess were all young, full of energy, very friendly, and having a good time. My knowledge of the English language was a little rusty by then, but they took it seriously to teach me the important things in life, like the names of Santa's reindeer.

That fall Marv invited me to many social functions on the base, and I was very impressed when I attended my first parade and he was the colour officer carrying the flag for the regiment. I had always been a big fan of brass bands, and they were playing military marches I could tap my toes to. I even owned the recommended clothing for women in attendance, suits and hats.

Shortly after that, Marvin informed me that he was planning to buy a red convertible Triumph TR 4 sports car. This was too good to be true. When he came to pick me up with the car, I knew I had found the man I wanted to spend my life with. For years I had longingly looked at photos of royalty in Europe in magazines driving their convertibles. I think it was in the genes from my dad to be attracted to cars, but our family didn't even have one while I was growing up.

After Christmas, when Marvin was not away taking courses or training, we spent most of our weekends together—Saturdays and Sunday afternoon and evenings. On Sunday morning I went to church. For my family, religion was very important. I was raised with good moral principles and to love my neighbour.

But something my family did not practice was affection, and I was craving it. So when Marvin was no longer shy, we kissed and hugged. He had not been raised in a religious family and we discussed the topic of God regularly. My understanding was that God created and cared for us. I was still living with my family when we returned from some of our outings late at night. A few times, when I walked into my bedroom, I found my aunt sitting on my bed in the dark waiting for me. Even though she prayed daily, she was always filled with anxiety. I believe it was a leftover from the war.

Shortly after my 22nd birthday I moved into an apartment of my own in a neighbouring town close to work. Now Marvin and I had some privacy, and we could spend time by ourselves getting to know each other better.

In the spring he invited me to my first formal dinner and dance. I was so excited. He announced that I would need a long dress and gloves and that one of the members of the British royal family would be attending. It was the regimental birthday with a day full of activities and celebrations. We went shopping together and, of course, I picked the dress that Marvin liked—dark green taffeta with shoulder straps.

The event was everything I dreamed of. The 30 officers looked stunning in their red uniforms, and all the ladies were in long gowns of every colour imaginable. A six-course dinner was served. By this time I knew most of the officers and their wives in attendance, and they often told stories about life in Canada. It sounded so interesting and so different from everything I had ever known. I was curious to find out about outhouses; I'd never seen one. Also people talked about the prairies and the long distances between cities. I thought it would be fun to drive for hours in the big beautiful cars. Again we danced into the night. I felt as if I was in a fairy tale.

One day in August, during an outing in the Triumph, Marv asked me, "Would you like to become Mrs. Dyck?"

I didn't hesitate. Of course my answer was yes. I didn't have to think twice about immigrating to Canada. I knew I would like it there. All my life it was my dream to get married and have 10 children because I'd spent so many lonely hours growing up. The next time we went to see my family we announced our engagement. Needless to say, they were upset to know that I would eventually live so far away. I pointed out to my aunt that she was the one who had encouraged me to be the date for Marvin when we met.

Our wedding on the base was a formal military affair beginning with the vows in the Catholic chapel "Our Lady of Canada," followed by a formal dinner and a dance to live music. All the officers, their wives, our teacher friends, my family, and some friends were in attendance. At midnight we left in our Triumph and our honeymoon began.

MONIKA DYCK-SCHNEIDER was born at the end of World War II in West Germany. Orphaned when she was three days old, she has written her memoirs about her survival against all odds and her childhood and youth in Germany. She and her Canadian husband and family live in British Columbia.

# Romance in the Northwest

### * * *

## PHYLLIS QUALLS FREEMAN

lushing, I watched as four college boys struggled with the bulky black trunk containing everything I'd need for my first year at college. They climbed two flights of stairs to the second floor of the girl's dormitory (Northwest Bible College, Minot, North Dakota), then down the hallway to my room. I regretted thinking a trunk was the main piece of luggage a college girl should own; yet, it felt gently dramatic. My sister, Dot, and I arrived on the Great Northern Railroad, so the trunk suited my idea of traveling by rail.

The guys positioned the trunk in my room and hung around as several other students gathered to welcome me. Dot, a second-year student, introduced me to each one. I only remember one name, Bill—the guy with the Wellington boots and a crew-cut. *I heard a guy had to use wax to get his hair to stand straight up.* His hair reminded me of a short-toothed comb.

Bill joked with Dot and tossed a faded blue cleaning cloth at her. Missing, it landed on the shoulder of my lavender cotton blouse. With a slight smile, I barely acknowledged his miss. Later, I discovered Bill was from a small town in Minnesota—a Western man. The boots added just enough height to make him six foot tall.

As we merged into college life, the students congregated into groups. I hung with Ann and Jack and a couple other students. Most of us were taxied to church services by teachers or students with vehicles. They also drove us downtown or to small congregations in surrounding cities. Most of those cities were at least 30 miles apart with rolling hills and a few farm houses between. We sang for the small congregations and critiqued student preachers.

I was on the work-study program in the school's office. An extra benefit was that I quickly got acquainted with everyone in the school.

Back in high school, my two guy friends were a little younger than myself. I was comfortable with them because there wasn't an expectation of dating. I'd only had a few dates, and they were with guys of meager communication skills.

Bill and a girl from South Carolina attended some events together, though later Bill told me they hadn't been dating at all—just hanging out. I hoped the guy with the boots and the curious smile noticed me; he was the only one I gave a second glance.

Another ministerial-hopeful student hung around my office and asked me to type a couple letters for him, and he bought Cokes for me at the student snack bar. He gazed at me a little too long and let it be known he came to college to search for a wife to join him in ministry. I was concerned he might ask me for a date; I wouldn't have obliged because I wasn't interested in his long-term plan.

Without my knowledge, a rumor wormed its way through the boy's dorm that a young man in our local church planned to take me out. I'd had no idea of his interest. He was strikingly handsome and a little older. His family was well established in town and in the church. I'm not sure how I would have responded if he'd called.

At first, Bill thought I was uninterested in him because I was careful not to be overconfident with guys. Even with that thought, Bill took the leap and asked me out. Our first date was on Thanksgiving Day.

When Bill asked if I'd go to the Thanksgiving service with him, I agreed. We caught a ride with a male staff member. As I stepped near to get into the back seat of the car with Bill, the dean of women kindly said, "Come sit up here with us, Phyllis."

So, on my first date with Bill I sat between two staff members. Bill and I did share a pew during the service, then we hurried to the car, and I quietly slipped into the back seat next to Bill. I had to smile to myself because I was with the cutest boy in the school. Bill was on the college basketball team and was one of the school's top ping-pong players. He played all sports with a vengeance, even our casual all-students' games. Dot vouched for him as a really good guy.

The school's vestibule had a little black book. Each student was required to *sign out* whenever they left the campus. If a girl and a guy went together, they had to have a chaperone. Perfect. Dot qualified, since she was an assistant to the women's dean and was usually available.

Winter in North Dakota wasn't anything like we'd experienced in Michigan. The temperatures plummeted lower, and snowstorms came more quickly and more severely. The close-by Mouse River froze in early winter, and the students ice-skated for weeks. I had ice skates, Bill borrowed a pair, and we often begged Dot to accompany us. It was good exercise, and it was quite proper to hold hands. Skating was a favorite activity for two college students who were falling in love.

A group of students planned to drive a hundred miles on a Sunday morning for church services in Bismarck.

The temperature was predicted to drop to 30 degrees below zero that Saturday night, and the guys knew one student's older vehicle might not start the next morning. Bill carefully wrapped a special cord around the battery to provide heat and plugged the cord into the porch light of a cottage on campus. Several guys rotated getting up throughout the night to start the car and let it run for a few minutes. The next morning we left without a crisis.

In the afternoon, the group was cautioned to head back toward Minot. It was heavily snowing with much more predicted. We groaned about having to leave without the *lunch* after evening service. The ladies of the Bismarck church never failed to have plenty of German and Swedish snacks for us when we visited. Their apple küchen (coffeecake) was my favorite.

The group left in good spirits but soon heavy snow blanketed the roads. Bill carefully followed the tracks of the cars ahead of us. We silently prayed for him. Eventually, he rolled down his window and stuck his head out to see the tire tracks since the windshield wipers did little good in the blizzard-like weather. The groups did arrive safely back in Minot.

I noted that Bill had a sincere, protective attitude toward me and other students and admired these good qualities. Each time Bill and I attended another event or church service, we felt more and more at ease with each other.

One evening Jack and Ann were in the lounge alone. Bill whispered, "Watch this." He pulled out a quarter and said to Jack, "I'll flip you for the lounge. Heads we win, tails you lose."

Jack said, "Okay."

Bill flipped the coin into the air and caught it in his hand, slapping it on his wrist, "Tails. You lose." Bill pulled that trick a couple of times, even letting Jack do the coin toss before they figured it out. In that lounge, Bill gave me his first sweet, warm kiss. I gave one in return.

I'd hoped to meet a guy like Bill, a guy I could respect for his Christian standards and who would cherish me. I felt blessed by Bill's solid family grounding. We talked about our dreams and our goals. When I looked into Bill's hazel eyes, I saw our future. When he held my hand, my whole body tingled. To me, there's still nothing more romantic than a man's arm around his girl or him holding her hand.

We are still in love after 53 years of marriage. Troubles? We faced many, but Bill is protector, lover, friend, and spiritual partner. He encouraged me to be all I could be.

Our three children gave us five grandchildren and two great-grandchildren.

Bill says the very first time he saw me was when I arrived with my mother to pick Dot up from the college the previous spring. He watched the blonde, blue-eyed girl from Michigan. Bill said he couldn't explain what happened next. "I looked at my roommate, Joel, nodded toward you, and stated, 'I'm going to marry that girl.'"


PHYLLIS QUALLS FREEMAN writes from Chattanooga, Tennessee. She has numerous articles and devotionals published in *Devotions, Secret Place, Reflections,* in several newspapers, and is on staff with Christian Devotions, **http://www.christiandevotions.us** as Prayer Coordinator and devotional writer.

**http://www.sanctuaryofhope.us**

# Love in the Time of Roller Skates

**\* \* \***

## SHIRLEY E. COLLINS

It was the roller-skating season in North Vancouver on the coast of British Columbia, and every girl wanted to be there for the gorgeous guys who whirled and stopped and whirled and stopped on their skates. These guys skated all year, every season, but for the girls who were beginners, it was a new season, a new experience, a new life.

I was just putting away the chairs at the end of the Hi C meeting in our church. It was never explained to me what Hi C meant, but it was a club I found so I would not be so lonely. My life was great, but I needed more.

At 16 I knew there was more to life than school, so my sister and I joined the church group. It was 1966.

My boyfriend, Vic, and his friend, Brian, were meeting me at the door after the chair stacking, and there they were! Oh, my gosh, Vic was so cute—dark hair, dark moustache, light skin. What else could a girl want?

His friend, Brian, also had dark features, but his olive skin was attractive to me because I was quite fair. He was so quiet; he just stared at me. I thought, *I must look pretty good.* That day I had on a turquoise "Poor Boy." It was a slightly ribbed short-sleeve knit that was so popular at the time, and boy did it fit snugly...maybe that's why they called it a "Poor Boy." I was gifted with a large chest and, of course, I'm sure, looking back later, that was what Brian was looking at.

Vic was a friendly guy with a great smile. He trusted everyone and had no idea his friend was looking at me in a way that other guys would feel jealous. His first thought was me. His first spoken words were, "Hey, Sheryl (he called me that instead of Shirley), this is my friend, Brian."

I found out later that Brian had just broken up with his girlfriend named Sheri-Lynn, so his hello was more a shocked jerk of the head, and then his body went stiff and he said a soft, "Hello." I think our names were too close for comfort for him.

Brian was going to be the driver on the weekend. He owned a sage green

Chevrolet with four doors, and he was taking a group of us to the roller-skating rink in North Van. I was included because I was Vic's girlfriend. I only know the details about his car because he was quite proud of it and talked about it before he drove the three of us home, his deep brown eyes sparkling as he dusted a spot.

The night we had planned to go roller skating came fast. I had just finished getting ready, and I stole a peek out of my bedroom curtain.

Brian's car was approaching my parents' driveway like a large shark: silent, and scary. I found it scary because my heart was beating fast, and all I could think about was Brian for the last week. I felt sorry for Vic because he had no idea what I was thinking, and he was too nice a guy to hurt. I had to put on an act to pretend, and that was scary for me. Yet I was taught to be genuine and honest.

Vic and I climbed into the backseat. Brian and another one of their mutual friends (I couldn't believe it; his name was Vic too) were in the front. Apparently, I was to be the only girl.

Vic and I necked in the back seat the whole time. Don't get me wrong. I am not "one of those girls," but kissing was allowed in my book. When we arrived at the arena I could see that all three guys were the guys that whirled and stopped, whirled and stopped on their skates. The songs in the '60s were rocking, and songs like "This Diamond Ring" by Neil Diamond blared from the speakers.

It was enough to send a girl reeling into romance.

As couples whirled by us on the hardwood of the arena, I kept watching for Brian. He stood off to one side and never seemed to ask a girl to skate. Vic and I skated with our arms around each other to the songs of the '60s as the disco ball twirled, making bright round shapes all over the floor.

The next few weeks were a blur with final exams at school.

Once the school year was over, the hot summer enveloped us, and that's when the house parties began. We continued to go skating, and the same scenario happened. Vic and I skated. Brian stood alone.

One night Vic was walking over to pick me up. He lived nearby with his mom and sister. He spoke little about his father. Vic was a bit of a soft touch and a nerd in tough guy's minds. I wasn't sure how the fight started but, between his house and mine, a few guys decided to rough him up, and he arrived with a bleeding nose and lip. My father saw him first and looked at him with contempt. Looking back, I'm not quite sure if my father really liked Vic. My mom and I ran to his aid with ice and a cold cloth. He lapped it up. I could see my dad's opinion set in the sternness of his face.

At the second house party of the summer, the windows were open, the curtains rustling, and Vic was asked by another girl to dance. That left Brian and I on the sidelines alone. It was then that a rock-and-roll couple having a blast twirled in front of me and knocked me over. Brian was sitting on a chair at the time, and I was standing. I was knocked right into his lap.

After the initial shock of it, I could then see the whole situation. Here I was, sitting on Brian's lap, right where I longed to be, and he was so moved by it that I could feel his body warm below me. We both looked at each other, and it was an instant connection, love at first sight (for those of us who believe in that).

Vic was still dancing, not quite tuned into what was happening. The few minutes the song was playing and I was sitting on Brian's lap was as though the world had stopped, and nobody else was in the room. Once the song finished playing, and just before Vic came back to our side of the room, Brian became very brave. He whispered five short words into my ear: "I am crazy about you."

The rest of the evening was like a haze. When we all went home and were dropped off, one by one, my head was still spinning.

Later that summer, I had to break it off with Vic. He was quite gallant about it and, contrary to what my father believed, he did have courage. It was after he found out how Brian and I felt about each other that he personally brought Brian over to the basement of my parents' house and offered him to me, then quietly backed out. That was how much Vic cared about me and my happiness.

To this day I think about Vic and that time of my life. Brian and I married and were together for 40 years. When Brian died at age 60, I tried to find out where Vic was. His mother answered the phone but did not remember me. She said Vic was married with one child and lived on Vancouver Island.

I will never forget the gorgeous guys who whirled and stopped and whirled and stopped at the roller-skating rink in North Vancouver in 1966.

SHIRLEY E. COLLINS, a retired grade-seven teacher, has two published books—one nonfiction and one fiction. She's an avid reader and movie watcher and, outside of running her dog, her joy is writing. Shirley says, "There is always a plot, a feeling, and a love story that everyone remembers. The love story, the soul of our being, tugs on the threads of our lives, keeping it taut and full of wonder."

# Second Chances and the Death Star

* * *

## Suzanne Reeves

"Who would ever want a woman like me?" I asked through tears at my friend's kitchen table. Recently divorced with a three-year-old daughter, I couldn't imagine a more undesirable dating prospect than me.

"A good man. A man who loves the Lord. That's who will want you," my friend comforted me. I nodded and mustered a feeble smile. I wasn't all that sure there were any of those kind of men left.

After four years of dating, five good years of marriage, and three more years of agony, the judge pounded his gavel and pronounced my marriage dissolved. In seconds I moved from being a Mrs. to a Divorcée. A thousand miles from my home. With a young child. A used-up woman who had to check the divorce box on the church questionnaire, with a house in need of major repairs, no solid job prospects, and an old arthritic cat. Now there's a man magnet if I've ever seen one.

After some healthy grieving and precious time with the Lord, I decided I was ready to date again. Surely I had some redeeming qualities. Qualities that would be desirable beyond just a dating charity case. I could mow the lawn; I loved football, and could speak Pig Latin. Well, it was a start. Armed with those assets and my best red lipstick, I began wading back into the dating pool.

Determined to do it right this time, I set out to find myself one of those good godly men my friend swore were still out there. My couples Sunday school class was not the best starting point as those men were taken. Neither was the singles group at my church. Everyone in it was old enough to remember Roosevelt being in office. The first Roosevelt.

After going on a date with the two single (and age-appropriate) guys at my church, I felt it was time to broaden the pond I was fishing in. And while the bar scene had many prospects, they didn't really fit the type of guy I was looking for in a mate. At all. Ever.

So I gave online dating a try. I answered question after question about my type, not my type, the type I wanted, and the type I would never get, so face reality and let it go, sister. I psychoanalyzed myself, examined my inner desires, drew up a diagram of the perfect man, sought the Lord, redid my perfect man diagram, and fed my aging cat vitamins. I was ready.

And believe it or not, the Lord brought several good godly men my way. I went on some dates, and we had fun. But although these men were nice, they just weren't the One.

And then one day (five years after my divorce,) I got an email from a guy named Rick. Our profiles were compatible, and he liked my smile. I consistently ran late, and he was always early. Perfect! He offered to take me to dinner, which I thought was a good sign. None of this *meet at a coffee shop and chat* stuff. I could do that with my friends! I took him up on his dinner offer, and we talked nonstop for over four hours and shut the restaurant down. Rick loved football, and he loved the Lord. He was divorced and had two kids of his own. My story didn't scare him one bit. He even pretended to be impressed with my Pig Latin.

Rick lived in Indianapolis, and I lived in the Chicago suburbs. He called me the very next day and asked if he could make the drive again the following weekend. I said yes, and he hasn't stopped driving the 209 miles door to door every weekend.

We got married on a beach in Mexico with our children at our side, surrounded by dear friends and family. Standing on a massive boulder, we said our vows with the mighty Pacific in the background. We wanted a visual image of placing our lives and our marriage on The Rock.

I knew what I wanted in a mate. But I also knew that God knew what I truly needed. I made out my list, but I left it open-ended with room for negotiation. I didn't want to miss the blessing of the right man because I was distracted looking for my idea of a perfect man.

Rick is 15 years older than me. I had put 10 as a good number on my list. He is neurotic about keeping things clean and in order. I live in a world of happy chaos. He is a retired United States Marine (served 21 years), and I am a free-spirited lover of all things colorful and artistic.

I imagined a romantic and hopefully dramatic wedding proposal. Somehow the real thing involved watching *Star Wars* on the couch with friends and my daughter. As Luke was destroying the Death Star, Rick brought out the ring, and suddenly we were engaged.

"Luke, use the Force."

"Really? Right now? Should we at least mute the TV?"

Rick is the logical one, and I think practicality is so overrated. He goes around fixing and cleaning everything for me. And I help him relax and wear pastel colors. We are just right for each other.

We have lamented many times how we wish we had found each other earlier in life. But we both know that God's timing is perfect. Rick is the man he is because of the life he has lived. He still suffers physically from a broken back, being wounded in combat in Beirut. He bears the scars of two failed marriages and an upbringing with an abusive father.

I grew up in a wonderful, loving Christian home. I was very close with my family, but being a dutiful wife, I left my family to be with my first husband. And then my first husband left me, and I couldn't go home.

Our stories are very different. But the outcome was the same. Long before we ever met, Rick and I were broken before the Lord. And that is what really matters. Not our pasts. Not our scars and not our mistakes. All that matters is our total dependence on God. The Lord picked us up in our suffering, dried our tears, and began to heal our wounds.

And then, when we were ready—when we were complete in Him—our Father introduced us to each other. I imagine God smiling as our online profiles found each other in His supernatural algorithm. Rick kissed me good night after that first date and later told me he couldn't stop touching his lips on the three-hour drive home.

Oh, how sweet are the blooms in the desert. The Lord has begun to restore the years the locusts have eaten. Rick is still covering the miles between our two cities (although we are hoping to be in the same household soon). As I worship the Lord in church with the man I love at my side, I am so very thankful. Rick loves me deeply and passionately. We are doing our best to make up for lost time. My friend knew what she was talking about after all. For I have found the one my heart desires. He is a good man. He loves me. And he loves the Lord.

And we have a date with the Death Star every year to celebrate.


SUZANNE REEVES is a misplaced Texan living near Chicago. Recently remarried, she is enjoying married life and hopes that, if she waits long enough, her wonderful husband will empty out the nasty vacuum cleaner bag so she doesn't have to.

**www.suzannereeves.com**

# The Choice

## * * *

## TERRI TIFFANY

I never went to redneck bars until that night. My younger sister was marrying a guy I thought was no good for her, so I figured a night out dancing and giving her the opportunity to meet someone new would persuade her to rethink her choice. Instead, I found myself rethinking my choice.

The two ex-servicemen quickly brought their drinks to our table and soon whisked us to the crowded dance floor. Bill was nice, but I couldn't get my eyes off his friend, who was dancing with my sister. Curt's sense of humor matched mine, and I was drawn to his boyish good looks and his Earth shoes. Yes, I had a thing for men who dressed nicely. If they couldn't take care of themselves, then how could they take care of the rest of their life?

Before I knew it, the night had ended and we said our good-byes—with my sister missing her fiancé even more. As we drove home, my thoughts kept turning to the man who had been talking with my sister and how I wished it had been me.

Three weeks later, I returned to The Bucket of Blood with another friend who said she needed a night out and had heard about the band playing. Normally, I wouldn't have gone again, but my boyfriend of two years had made plans with his friends that night as well. His friends weren't people I thought were the best of influence on him, but I didn't mind. After all, Mike and I had talked of marriage and, in a few weeks, when I graduated from college, we would put our plans in order. Mike had been a good friend and a steady, dependable guy even though I found myself taking him for granted on more than one occasion.

I dressed in my favorite pink sweater and my new jeans. A part of me felt guilty that I was going to such lengths to look my best and Mike wasn't with me. Our relationship had come to that, though—we seemed to spend more time with our friends than with each other.

The bar was packed, but we finally found a table near the half wall in the back. Then I saw him—the man from before—Curt. I remembered his name and how he'd made me feel when he'd talked with us that night. I'm normally a shy girl, but for some reason God must have given me a nudge. I reached out as he passed our table and said "Hi," surprising not only him but me as well.

That's all it took. He recognized me and slid across the table with a huge smile. My heart raced as I considered my actions, but I couldn't stop. When he asked me to dance, I rose eagerly and went into his arms as a song I knew played. We danced for over an hour until finally he asked if we could step outside to talk. He had trouble hearing inside, he said, from being a trumpet player in the service.

A musician. Already he impressed me.

But I have this rule. I never leave an establishment with someone I don't know. Besides, I was practically engaged. I also have a healthy fear of strange men. But something about Curt and the way he asked tugged me to the exit. Soon I found myself walking along the highway in the dark listening to him sharing his dreams and hopes.

He took my number and the next morning, I knew what I had to do. I called Mike and told him I had to break up with him. I didn't want to hurt him any worse than I had already.

"We've been together two years," he said, tears in his voice.

Was I a heartless creature? Something pushed me on. "I think we aren't right for each other. I'm so sorry."

I cried for an hour and then I waited.

And waited. Days passed and no phone call. I was starting to think maybe I was wrong about Curt—that maybe he hadn't been serious. I kept replaying his words and how he'd told me about his life and desires. Had I made a mistake? Maybe he'd lost my number and we'd never connect. Was I destined to have met the man of my dreams and then never see him again?

"He'll call," my older sister assured me. "You said you connected. Give it more time."

I tried to concentrate on my final semester, but the memory of that special night continued to intrude. Maybe I hadn't felt God's nudge. Maybe I was wrong about what I'd felt.

Two weeks passed. The phone rang as I was eating dinner at our kitchen counter.

"Hey, it's me, Curt. Would you like to go to dinner with me next week?"

"What took you so long?" I said, immediately regretting my words.

He explained how he had rolled his car that night, and it was still in the shop. He'd pick me up with his parents' car, if that was fine with me.

Anything he said was fine with me.

He was two hours late getting to my apartment since his parents' car also broke down.

"Are you hungry still?" Curt said as he stood in my doorway looking as handsome as I remembered him.

I said I was starving so he took me to a nearby Italian restaurant. I don't remember eating one bite. His plate never emptied as well.

I tell people I believe in love at first sight. I know I fell in love with Curt the first time I saw him. He later told me he felt the same way. We spent all our free time together getting to know each other. It took him two weeks to kiss me good night.

Two months later he proposed. He asked me like he might propose a business deal. One by one he raised his fingers and counted off the reasons why it would be good if we married.

"I love you, Terri," he finally said in the darkened car.

That's the only reason I cared about. I wrapped my arms around his neck and sealed the deal with a kiss. I'd met the man who cared about my hopes and dreams and who I knew would fulfill them all.

We married less than nine months after meeting—a month after my sister married the man of her dreams.

This year we will celebrate our 35th wedding anniversary.

I haven't stopped listening to God's small still voice when it comes to my husband and our choices, and he hasn't either. Together we've stepped into our future, offering each other the opportunity to take chances with our dreams.

Our marriage has been an adventure filled with more ups and downs than I care to count, but through it I all, I remember. I remember that special night where I made a choice to change the path I was headed down. I took a chance. I listened to that voice telling me, *"Terri, speak up. This is the partner I've chosen for you."*

I'm not so shy anymore. Maybe it's because I have my lifelong love at my side.

TERRI TIFFANY counseled adults, owned a Christian bookstore, and now resides in Texas with her husband. Her work has appeared in magazines, Sunday school take-home papers, and anthologies such as *Chicken Soup for the Soul* and *Blue Mountain Arts*.

http://terri-treasures.blogspot.com/

# An Unexpected End
## Philip and Aeryn

\* \* \*

### VAL HALLORAN

From the first time the beautiful, dark-eyed brunette walked into his Sunday school class, Philip was surprised by the intensity of attraction that he felt for this girl whom he had not yet met, but somehow sensed would one day become his wife. Little did he know then just how long and difficult the journey would be.

After the class ended, Philip was quick to introduce himself to Aeryn and was encouraged to discover that she seemed equally interested in getting to know more about him. Before much time had elapsed, Philip asked Aeryn for her phone number, and they began getting acquainted over the phone and on internet chats. Despite the fact that Phil was only 18 years old and Aeryn 17, it took just a couple of weeks before they both believed they had found their future spouses. That was August of 2009.

As months went on, Philip's interest in Aeryn was consistent, but Aeryn was gradually finding interest in other things that drew her away from spending time with Philip. Aeryn started playing soccer on Monday nights with another church group and began forming most of her friendships with people in that group, while spending time with Philip seemed to become less and less of a priority. Meanwhile, wanting more definite direction for his life than his first semester in college had provided, Philip decided to join the Marine Corps. Becoming a Marine would not only give Phil career direction, but would also put him in a better position to marry Aeryn sooner, even though she told him before he left for boot camp that she did not yet feel ready for marriage.

After Philip left for 13 weeks of boot camp, Aeryn's attention began to wander to things that made her uncertain about her feelings for Phil. Realizing that it wasn't fair to keep Philip in the dark about her changing feelings, right before he was due to graduate from boot camp, she sent him a "Dear John" letter, timing it so he wouldn't receive the bad news before he completed the final, grueling, three-day "Crucible," required to earn the title of US Marine. Aeryn knew it would be a hard time for Phil to receive her letter, but she hoped that his pride in becoming a Marine would soften the blow.

Fortunately, the challenges of his training did provide a different focus for Phil over the following months during which Aeryn struggled to learn the meaning of true love.

Something unexplainable had caused Aeryn to change over the months that finally led to her break-up with Phil. She not only had no feelings left for him, but following their break-up, she expressed obvious disdain whenever Philip's or his family's names were mentioned . During the first couple of weeks of Phil's career in the Marine Corps, he tried to contact Aeryn, just wanting to talk things out so he could have some closure and understanding of what had happened; but she seemed unwilling to have conversation or contact with him.

As months passed, Aeryn seemed distant from everyone who really cared about her. She began to pass most of her time with the friends she met at the new church, or at school, spending little time at home or at her family's church. Her parents tried not to worry, hoping Aeryn's behavior was only her way of trying to establish her own adult identity. But after a while, they began to suspect that Aeryn was attracted to a young man named Mark, whom she met at the church where they both played soccer. Upon being questioned, Aeryn denied having any attraction to him and said they were just good friends. But after going on a mission trip where Mark was part of the team, Aeryn later admitted that she and Mark had grown to like each other. She justified not discussing things with her parents by saying that she and Mark had decided on their own that they were not in a good position to have a serious relationship. That was in August of 2010.

The weeks and months passed with no change as far as Aeryn's interest in even talking to Philip, much less in restoring any type of relationship with him. Phil had long since stopped trying to contact her but kept in touch with her mother. Even when his family would get together with Aeryn's family, she would make deliberate plans to be somewhere else so she didn't have to see any of them. By all outward appearances, any hope for a future between them seemed to be a far-fetched fantasy.

Then, just before Christmas of 2010, news came that would, from a human perspective, completely shatter all hope of there ever being reconciliation between Philip and Aeryn. As her family was preparing for the arrival of her brother and sister, who were coming home for Christmas, Aeryn asked her parents if she and Mark could meet to talk with them. They wondered why Mark would be involved in the discussion, since he and Aeryn had supposedly stopped all communication.

Regardless, nothing could have prepared them to hear the announcement that was the purpose for that meeting. Shortly after Mark arrived at their home, the announcement was made that Aeryn was expecting Mark's baby. Everyone sat in stunned silence at first. The initial disbelief, anger, shame, and confusion that followed the announcement quickly overshadowed any joyful anticipation of the upcoming family reunion. Tears were shed and difficult words exchanged in an attempt to understand how this had happened and where they should go from there. Aeryn knew that her behavior disappointed both God and her family, but she had allowed herself to gradually slip away from accountability and from the counsel of those who loved her, leaving herself vulnerable to the deception that resulted in her condition.

But by turning to a merciful God and a loving family to forgive and guide her, Aeryn would learn something of the depth of God's grace during the painful days that followed. She and her family would be given a firsthand opportunity to see God's redemptive power and mercy toward those who seek His forgiveness and help.

Many agonizing decisions had to be made following that devastating announcement. While there is always joy in the anticipation of a new life entering the world, the circumstances surrounding that event were now complicated by choices that had been made outside of God's plan. For the baby's sake and because Mark and Aeryn said they "loved each other," they at first said they were going to get married.

But shortly after Aeryn's pregnancy was announced, Mark admitted he was having second thoughts about marriage. Without Mark's willingness to unreservedly commit to marriage, Aeryn was no longer allowed to maintain regular contact with him—not only to protect her from further failure, but so that God's will in the matter could be prayerfully discerned.

In the meantime, Philip sensed that things weren't right. Even though he was stationed in another state, he contacted Aeryn's mother to see how she was doing. Naturally, when the painful news was shared with him, he was devastated. But surprisingly, as when he first laid eyes on Aeryn, he was filled with unexplainable love for her. He felt compassion for her, rather than the anger that one would expect from a man in his position. Philip's feelings, along with ongoing prayers from both sets of parents, gave hope that things might eventually work out between them after all. But in order not to coerce, or influence Aeryn, these hopes were not made known to her.

Just weeks after the baby's birth, unaware of both families' desires, Aeryn surprised her parents by asking permission to write a letter of apology to Philip for the things she had done to hurt him. Though inwardly delighted, they nonchalantly gave permission for her to send the letter.

During those months of shame and solitude, Aeryn had the opportunity to realize that Mark's "love" had been self-gratifying, while Philip's was patient and unconditional.

Philip surprised himself by his immediate willingness to accept Aeryn's apology letter, wondering during their time of separation how he would react if Aeryn ever did return to him. But by grace, God had prepared Philip to demonstrate His unconditional love and forgiveness toward Aeryn.

After more times of prayer and talking things through, their love for one another was beautifully rekindled. God's leading was soon made clear, and both families were delighted to give their blessing for Philip and Aeryn to be married the day after Thanksgiving of 2011.

God, through Philip's willingness to forgive, graciously granted Aeryn a second chance to learn the difference between infatuation and genuine love. Today, Aeryn and baby Bella (unhappy in this picture, but happy in life), are enjoying the security of a home provided by a devoted husband and father, all because of a loving and merciful Heavenly Father.

VAL HALLORAN, wife of 33 years and mother to eight children (including Aeryn) and 13 grandchildren, is also a songwriter who has produced three recording projects of original songs, as well as songs recorded by other artists.

**www.valhalloran.com**

# In Sickness and In Health

### * * *

## VALERIE D. BENKO

Tears well as the silver 12-gauge precision-glide needle dangles threateningly above the top of my thigh like an angry stinger.

The room begins to fade as my brain screams for oxygen. I force the air I'm holding out of my lungs, and my tiny kitchen comes back into focus. A memory of a magazine article about the calming effects of nitrous oxide sparks in my brain—inhale deeply to release it. I inhale deeply, but now I'm back to holding my breath.

"You can do this," my husband coaxes me in his soothing baritone voice.

I think of all the diabetics who inject several times a day. *But theirs aren't intramuscular....*

He reminds me that it's just one shot, once a week. "You're bigger than the needle."

His pep talk is slowly calming my fears. I'm not a needle-phobe. Anytime I have to get a flu or allergy shot I politely roll up my sleeve or show a little hip. If it hurts, it's over so fast I don't even have time to react.

So why is my hand quivering now? *Because I'm the one who has to do it.*

As I stare at the pointed end of the syringe, all I can think about is the day my husband playfully dropped one of my needles onto the kitchen table and it stuck in the wood. *It's that sharp!*

He is patiently sitting on the chair next to me, watching, soft blue eyes focused on the needle, waiting for the precise moment I inject and purge the clear liquid from the vial. He always recaps the needle when I pull it out and drops it into the waiting Sharp's container. Then he either high-fives me or gives me a hug or a kiss, or all three.

We're a team—husband and wife, patient and honorary nurse. It doesn't matter if it is my turn to give myself the injection or his; we always do the steps together. If it wasn't for his loving support and humor, I don't know if I ever would have survived this far into my treatment.

Two months before my 30th birthday, I sat staring at the tiled floor of an examination room with my husband sitting beside me in the hard plastic chair as my neurologist delivered the fateful news, "You have MS."

Those three words changed mine and my husband's future forever. We had only been married for three years and in an instant he went from being my spouse to being my caregiver, but it also gave us answers as to why my legs kept going numb and why I was forgetting how to do things.

Multiple sclerosis is a neurological auto-immune disease that affects the central nervous system and to date there isn't a cure. The disease is progressive, and medicine is delivered to the body through injections.

The diagnosis took over a year and involved MRIs, enough bloodwork to make vampires foam at the mouth, a spinal tap, and an EMG. Walking became difficult due to numb feet and legs. My husband had to hoist me up into our Jeep because I was no longer strong enough to pull myself in. He became my chauffeur as my vision faded to a white cloud. As the nerve signal was lost in my broken body it affected my bladder, slowed my cognitive function, and brought on depression. I missed three months of work while my body tried to heal.

My husband remained my cheerleader and teammate. During that difficult time, he drove me everywhere, made dinner every night, read things off of the TV, and bathed me when I had an IV stuck in my arm for almost a week. He always reminded me that things were going to get better, no matter how bad they seemed. His gentle jokes about my situation made me smile. His warm hugs and tender kisses were as healing as the medicine flowing through my veins.

On one particularly bad symptom day I was feeling really depressed and told him I felt like a fraud. He had married me under the guise that I was a healthy young woman with a long life in front of her. Now I was sick and dependent. I told him if he wanted to leave I would understand. Instead, he pulled me to him and said, "...in sickness and in health. I do."

I didn't think it was possible to fall in love twice with the same man. But I did. He had my heart the first day we met when he came into my place of employment to use the ATM and instead got trapped by mutual friends who wanted us to meet. I'll never forget how red his face was and how he stumbled through his words.

Five years into our relationship now, he held me in his strong arms, telling me he would always be there and that things would be okay. I fell in love with him all over again. In an age where people were divorcing quicker than they say "I do," he was standing by our sacred vows.

We have the type of love that some people search for their whole lives and never find. It's the type of love that classic fairytales are built on. We didn't "settle" for each other, we loved each other with our hearts wide open and that has made all the difference in our relationship.

After my symptoms faded and I was back to work part-time, he sat with me in the exam room as my neurologist decided one intramuscular injection a week would be better for me than smaller shots multiple times during the week. Since I wasn't confident I was even going to be able to stick a needle in my leg, I agreed.

The company that makes my medicine sent a nurse to our home to teach us how to properly inject. Although my husband was as nervous as I was, we took turns poking a needle into a Nerf ball and making jokes to calm our fears. We decided I would inject into the top of my thighs and he would take the two weeks when the injection went into the side of my thighs so I could lay down and relax.

That was nine months ago. So why am I reluctant to stick this one-inch long needle into my thigh now?

Because no matter how many times I do this, it never gets easier. There is always the anxiety that wraps me in its grip as I worry I may feel the needle. My stomach twists in knots and sometimes bile rises. Even if the injection goes well, I often suffer from ill effects of the medicine. And he's always there for that too. Covering me with a blanket when my body is racked with chills, helping me battle through a raging fever, and getting me ibuprofen when my muscles ache.

My husband is aware of my anxious state. The tears are running freely now and blurring my vision. I keep the skin pulled taunt on my thigh with the fingers on my left hand like the nurse taught me so the needle doesn't meet resistance. He offers to do it for me, reminding me that he'll do it every week if it makes it easier. He'll carry that burden so I don't have to. He's brave and he won't let me quit.

I smile. Having him beside me is all the strength I need to complete the task. I wipe my tears and inject.

In sickness and in health, we do.

VALERIE D. BENKO is a writer from western Pennsylvania where she works full-time as a Communications Specialist. She is a frequent contributor to *Chicken Soup for the Soul* and has had her personal stories published in other anthologies, e-books, and online.
http://valeriebenko.weebly.com
www.letterstoms.blogspot.com

# Living Alone Together

\* \* \*

## STANLEY L. KLEMETSON

I
t is dark as I fly into Lake Charles in April to wrap up the academic year so that I can return back to you. The sky is filled with clouds with lights shining through, here and there. Each light brings back a specific memory of our 50 years together. We have lived separately several times, and yet we always felt we were together as we shared each other's experiences by mail, telephone, e-mail, and, more recently, by texting. When you returned home last May I thought that we would be separated for only a few weeks, but family needs kept you there when I had to return to teach another year in Louisiana. I have been thankful for our visits every month and the long Christmas break.

I remember the February night that Frank introduced us. I was 17 years old, and Frank asked me to double-date with him for the Valentine's Day Dance. Since I did not have a girlfriend, he said that he would introduce me to the prettiest girl that he knew. With our guitars loaded into the back of my father's old pickup truck we started down a paved street, but soon ended up on a steep dirt road leading to your home on the top of a mountain. Frank led me through the trees until we found your front door. He knocked and the door opened slowly. There you stood, outlined by the light behind you. You were beautiful with your pretty face, long brown hair that lay on the shoulders of your pink mohair sweater. You were easy to talk to, and you even showed us the black widow spider you had captured that day. We went to play guitars with friends that night, but I think I spent most of the evening just looking at you.

The day for our date finally arrived, and we picked you up in my father's better looking car. You were beautiful that evening. I held your hand as we walked up to the youth center in the residential neighborhood. The lights were low. The dance floor was crowded, but that did not bother us as we danced the fast songs and the slow, and I was careful not to let you go. We talked and talked that evening. There was so much to know about you. When

I drove you home, I took you to your door but did not want to let you go. A short kiss good night and you were gone behind your door.

In the following months, we had long telephone conversations and weekend dates with movies, picnics, swimming at the beach, and long drives through the winding tree-covered roads. But we were young and we separated when you turned me down for my senior class party. I did not know until later that it was only because you did not have a dress for the party. If we could have only talked about it, I might taken you somewhere else that night.

Fortunately, in a few months my father and I started to build a small store on the road leading to your home. One day you dropped by. After you left, my father asked why I was not dating a nice girl like you. He was right. In a few weeks I hosted an after graduation beach party for my high school friends, and I invited you. On the beach I played my guitar and sang songs with you. We started to date again.

Remember when we had been dating for over a year and I gave you a friendship ring? How did I know it would turn your finger green! I corrected that mistake by buying you an emerald birthstone ring to replace it. One evening, when you were almost 18 and we were together, I stopped the car downtown. You said that you would wait in the car, but I said that you couldn't because we were going to buy you an engagement ring. Thankfully, you got out of the car and came with me. I don't recommend this approach, because you only get engaged once.

When we decided to marry, we also discussed we wanted to be included in our marriage. We wanted to have at least four children, and we wanted to make sure that we faithfully attended church together. We had set our marriage date for the following summer, but now that we were committed to each other we bought a trailer for our first home and filled it with dishes and other supplies. You moved into the trailer with a girlfriend, but after a month we decided that we were prepared and there was no reason to wait until next summer.

On October 19th we married in a small church wedding. With a $100 from our fathers we went on a three-day honeymoon and rode the merry-go-round in Golden Gate Park, fed the deer in Big Basin Park, and drove the 17 mile drive in Carmel. It was a great start to our marriage. After all these years I still like the monthly celebrations of our marriage on the 19th.

We were happy as husband and wife, but soon we wanted more. We wanted to be a father and mother. I held you as you cried because you were bleeding and would have a miscarriage with our first child. It was a difficult experience that you would have several more times. We were so happy to have our first child, a son, morning sickness, caesarean section and all. Fatherhood, motherhood, brought us such joy. There was so much to learn and I was proud of you as you guided us through the experience. Little did we know that we would have six children, watch them grow up, and have them bring us many grandchildren.

As a university professor, we had the opportunity to travel. Remember our summer in Oak Ridge, Tennessee? We lived a popup travel trailer with our four children in the TVA camp ground. Our son was invited to go to Scout camp in the Great Smoky Mountains. One moment that really stands out to me was the dinner we had with another family. They asked what my goals were, and I started to talk about professional goals when they stopped me and asked, "No, what are your spiritual goals?" Throughout our married life we have gone back to that question many times as we made decisions about how we wanted to live our lives during this mortal existence.

The road we travel is not always straight. Remember when I had to take a job in California and leave you at home for a short time? It turned into a year, but we e-mailed frequently and I came home every few weeks. Finally we decided that we had been apart too long. I found a job in Auburn so we could live together again.

This time we thought that it would be different when I found a job in Louisiana and you came with me. Little did we know that, after a year, you would have to return home to take care of family needs. However, separations can also bring some blessings. I took a poetry class and started to write poems to you to express my love for you and how much I missed you. You were my muse. I remember one moonlight night when I thought that you and I were sharing the same moon. That started a round of texting as we shared our thoughts about your snow-covered mountains and my warm sun and alligators. It was that night that I decided to start looking for a job closer to you and our family.

Now this separation is coming to an end. We have lived separately several times, but were never truly alone. We knew we loved one another and our family. Our lives have been filled with memories together, more than we thought possible when we married. Now it is time to be together again.

STANLEY L. KLEMETSON, Ph.D., is an Associate Dean of the College of Technology and Computing at Utah Valley University. He is a member of the Utah League of Writers, but his interest in fiction and poetry started with the Bayou Writers Group in Lake Charles, Louisiana.

# Love from the Cradle to the Grave
## Willie and Virdie

\* \* \*

## GLEN DAVENPORT

The year was 1920. The kids were 12 and 18. He asked, "Will you marry me?"

She answered, "I guess I could."

Tears of remembrance fell as my dad's thoughts went back nearly six decades to recall his and my mom's love story. The marriage was a match made in Heaven and lasted until the Lord called him home 58 years later.

A man named Marion came into the area from Glasgow, Kentucky, to work at a saw mill. He married a local girl named Lucy, who gave him two little girls before she passed away with a common disease (Tuberculosis, then called "consumption"). The girls were four years old and two years old at the time of their mother's death, and the four-year-old died a couple of years later for reasons unknown to us.

A few years later Marion was shot and killed. The younger of the two girls, Virdie, was left alone, orphaned at the age of nine. She had no legal guardian but lived most of three years with an aunt and uncle in Crab Orchard, Tennessee. There were times when she was shuttled back and forth between her relatives in Crab Orchard and those in Glasgow via passenger train. A note pinned to her dress told the conductor where to drop her off and who would pick her up. It appears that she was not well cared for. One uncle was quite bossy with her, so she lived more like a servant than a pitiful orphan.

A young man named Willie, who probably worked with Marion in the log woods, knew some things about the family before tragedies struck their home. Willie, an 18-year-old who lived at home with his mother, had compassion for the young girl and was interested in every conversation that included her. Young Willie was bringing his team of mules home after a day in the log woods when he passed by the home where Virdie was staying. He saw her sitting, crying, on the edge of the porch. Touched by the sight, he halted his mules to inquire about her grief.

The story is blurred, but it seems that her uncle had slapped her for not doing everything she was assigned to do or perhaps the chores weren't done the way he wanted them done. The incident was very upsetting to her. Life offered no pleasures in the home of her uncle. She wished she could go home or somewhere else. Her complaint and tears disturbed Willie deeply, but there was nothing he could do about it...unless he told her that he would take her home, and she could live with him and his mother.

But, he insisted, "We would need to get married." Then he promised, "If you marry me, I will see to it that no man will ever lay a hand on you again." Then he asked, "Would you want to do that?"

Her answer was a nonchalant, "I guess I could."

So, without one single date or evening out, plans for a wedding developed rather quickly. He and his mother went down to the General Store and

purchased enough broadcloth (blue surge) to make the 12-year-old girl a dress to get married in and a pair of patented-leather shoes, size two. Willie's mother made the dress and helped with the wedding arrangements. There was a railroad track near the store that was used as much by pedestrians as it was for the train. They were to meet a preacher somewhere on the railroad track and there they would exchange vows. So, Willie and Virdie were married on November 26, 1920. His mother was very helpful, teaching the little girl how to sew, cook, and do all household chores. Willie built them a four-room house out in the country. His mother lived with them and helped the teenage mother rear her children (later, the kind older woman died in 1933).

Willie and Virdie's first child was born in March before Virdie turned 14 in April. My mom gave birth to 16 children, eight boys and eight girls, and lived seven years after Dad's death. He died at the age of 76. She died at the age of 77. As of this date (2012) the family descending from the pair numbers almost 400 (including in-laws). Following is their story told in a poem/song.

## Willie and Virdie's Love Song

In a way it's very pretty. In a way it's very sad.
In a way it's perfect love, manifested through my dad.
I've always had a vision and wished I could write it out,
To tell our family through the ages what their life was all about.
There was a certain characteristic in this man called Dad,
Who took an orphan girl and gave her all he had.
He took that lonely little girl and raised her from a child
She was twelve when they got married so their oats were never wild.
Dad never had any other girl and she no other man.
Their love would stand the tests of time; even a 58-year span.
They started having children when both were very young
They ended up with 16 kids before their love song was sung.
Their lives were dedicated to each other and their kids.
They seemed to have us on their minds no matter what they did.
Dad worked a job to pay the bills, and Mom kept up the house.
She made our clothes and sowed the quilts and fed our hungry mouths.
Dad showed us how to tend the fields and cut the heating wood.
Mom taught us how to baby-sit and behave the way we should.
They raised their children near the woods and on a very small farm.
They never had the wealth of some but that caused us no harm.
We were allowed to do-our-thing and go where the Spirit led us.
Some did business or nursing jobs, and some turned out as preachers.
I think a lot about how things might have been.
If they had been lazy, unconcerned, and run out from the scene,
the world would not have been as good as it is this very day,
And if they had not raised us in church and taught us how to pray.
With near 400 in our family, God has shown how well He cares.
We have suffered no more than two dozen deaths in over 100 years.
Will the circle be unbroken when we stand in Heaven fair?
You can rest assured they instilled the faith it will take to get us there.
They could have been rich in houses and lands;
They could have had wealth untold.
But they both loved kids and invested in us.
The story is told in their clothes.

GLEN DAVENPORT, number 12 in a family of 16 children, lives in Crossville, Tennessee, and serves as the president of the Willie Davenport Family Reunion that began in 1955 and continues strong unto this date. He received his Ph.D. in Theology from Eastern Baptist Seminary near Cincinnati, Ohio, and served as an instructor for more than 10 years. He is married with two sons, two daughters-in-law, and four grandchildren, a pastor for more than 40 years, a published author with six books to his credit and a member of the Wright Touch Inspirational Writers Group in Fairfield Glade, Tennessee.

# A Love for
# More Than a Lifetime

* * *

## SUSAN SCHREER DAVIS

He saw me in a church and pictured marrying me. That's how we met, my boy's father and I. We didn't speak that day. In fact we didn't talk for several weeks. But our life together began when I walked into St. Philip Benizi Catholic Church shortly after getting my first traffic ticket.

I "failed to stop" in south Atlanta while serving as part of a renewal team coordinated by my Presbyterian father. My dad started organizing teams when I was twelve but never crossed the denominational divide until spring of my senior year in high school—the only year I opted out of the school musical.

I'd been promised a lead role that year, but challenges from the previous show kept me from auditioning. I couldn't fully explain why. I just felt like there was something more.

That something more led me to St Phillips in early April the next spring—the same weekend as the play. I helped with a few youth events and accompanied my younger brother, Mark, at the Sunday afternoon concert. But not being Catholic, I often felt out of place. By the time I entered the sanctuary after getting that ticket, I had puffy, red eyes.

And that's when Jason saw me—that's when the artist was intrigued.

When I played the piano for Mark, his interest grew. I later learned he spent the next hour wondering what it would be like to be an artist married to a musician. The thought never left, so within a week he took action.

Since Jason had sung with the same choir my brother represented, he decided to send him a donation for his upcoming tour. He called the church, asked for Mark's address, and crafted letters to both of us. Within days he dropped them in the mail.

I was in Nashville the day they arrived, auditioning at Vanderbilt's Blair School of Music. I called home after the audition to tell my mom I'd been accepted. She replied with typical mom enthusiasm and then added, "A letter came in the mail today with a donation to your brother. It also had an envelope with these words written on it: *Please give this to whoever played the piano for Mark.* Do you want me to open it?"

Not shy I blurted, "Sure!"

As I stood at an airport pay phone, waiting for a return flight, Mom read:

I've had some trouble trying to compose this letter so it won't sound too strange. I saw you at St. Phillips on Sunday and wanted to speak to you—but had to leave early. I sang with the Boy Choir years ago, so it was easy to help your brother out. Getting an address was so simple I had trouble finding arguments not to write this letter, however strange it may seem. I would like to talk to you. Even if I looked for a number I wouldn't know who to ask for—so I'll give you mine. This really isn't as silly or as much a generic pick-up as it may sound. Please call—it's relatively painless.

*Relatively painless.* Those last words got to me. So I called.

I learned that Jason attended the Atlanta College of Art and Design and wanted to paint pictures for a living. He was older than me and totally different from anyone I'd met—which made me nervous. But I told him he could call again. And in time he did.

I was busy with graduation events. But he was patient and, within six weeks, we went on our first date. As we drove to the Renaissance Festival, I mentioned I was looking for a summer job. Jason encouraged me to call his boss. Since he airbrushed T-shirts at *Six Flags over Georgia* and was one of their most talented and reliable artists, his reference alone got me a cashier position in the airbrush stands.

Two weeks after graduation, I put on my first uniform and entered unfamiliar territory where I leaned on his expertise and strength.

He was different in his element, more relaxed and self-assured. The tall, lanky, blue-eyed artist put me at ease and won my respect, creating almost any T-shirt a customer ordered. But when he walked me to my car in mid-June and asked if he could kiss me good night, I still wasn't ready. I liked him but was always cautious with my kisses.

He called me the next day—on Father's Day—and asked if he could come over. I knew something important was up since he asked so soon after the awkward ending. When he arrived a few hours later, we went for a walk.

"I've been thinking a lot since last night," he started. "If our relationship isn't supposed to be romantic then I have to figure out what it's about. Ever

153

since I first saw you, I felt there was something different about you and I want to understand it."

I didn't know to say. No one had ever described me that way. So I kept listening, and he kept talking.

He told me about disappointments in high school. A competition lost. Stolen artwork never found. A detention notice turned into a mark on his permanent record. He rebelled by wearing a vampire cape and fangs with his tux to prom and hoped things would change in college.

During Thanksgiving break of his freshman year, however, his parents noticed a slight pull to his eye. An image study done on one of the first MRI machines in Atlanta a few weeks later revealed a brain stem tumor. One doctor gave him six months to live.

But after months of radiation treatments, the tumor stabilized. And, three years later, he was walking in a light summer drizzle with me, trying to make sense of it all.

Having never talked to someone who had faced serious illness, I fumbled for words. So he continued, "All I know is that it's like there's a light inside of you; a light that seems to come from your faith. And I want to understand God the way you do."

We stood under a lamp post at the end of my drive way, damp from a heavy mist. I still didn't know what to say.

"Faith is simple to me," I tried. "My family has always gone to church. So believing God's love is bigger than the problems we face makes sense. I don't know how to make it real for you especially after the hard things you've faced. But I just believe He works things out in the end."

We parted as friends without solving his life dilemma. But within a month, he asked me out again. I well remember the moment I looked over at him as he drove to a restaurant that night and all my reservations melted away. He'd never treated me unkindly for putting off his advances, and as we worked side by side in the airbrush shops, our friendship had grown instead. The artist was mine for the taking, and everything in me suddenly wanted him.

We married three years later and had two boys before the tumor started growing again. I watched him breathe his last and step from here to eternity only six and half years after committing our lives forever. But we were both forever changed in that short time.

I needed the artist as much as he needed me and discovered the depths of my creativity once I lived around his. He encouraged me to write, and during his illness, helped me overcome my inner critic and compose songs. As the tumor grew, my faith and reassurance that God's goodness would prevail gave him strength to keep walking till he reached heaven's door.

After work one day during our first summer together at the park, Jason drove me to court to pay the traffic ticket. Before we walked in, he handed me a covered frame. He'd painted my first gift—a butterfly with a favorite verse, Jeremiah 29:11: "'For I know the plans I have for you,' declares the Lord, 'plans to prosper you and not to harm you, plans to give you hope and a future.'"

God brought us together for a plan and a purpose, a plan with a future that's different than what we wanted, but still filled with hope. Our together life transcended the typical Hallmark card 50-year marital dreams and served as a one-act play instead; a one act that continues to make a difference in the grand scheme of things today.

He saw me in a church and pictured marrying me. And his legacy—and the love we shared—still live on.

SUSAN SCHREER DAVIS has published stories in Focus on the Family magazines and recorded two CDs of her own music. She teaches voice and piano, co-owns *Go Fish Clothing and Jewelry* (located on the Marietta Square) with her husband, and relishes being a mom and wife.

www.susanschreerdavis.com
www.susanschreerdavis.blogspot.com

# A World of Two

*** 

## KRISTI PAXTON

Guilt propelled me up the ladder to the roof where Denny, my husband of 38 years, hammered on ice and shoveled chunks onto the ground below. The job was too big for one person. Ice had formed a dam at roof's edge, and we needed to chip it away to stop the drips coming into our house.

When either of us started sliding, we simultaneously gasped. It struck me that we constituted a marriage metaphor—hammering away at the bad stuff, often alone, but side by side, ready to hold each other up or drag each other down.

We decided to take turns making 10 violent hacks apiece. "Can you spell condominium?" I asked, trying to lighten the mood.

My thoughts drifted from the roof to sweeter times. How did we get from tenderness to treachery? If I described our journey with words, would I write a love story or an accident report? Any official document would chronicle a series of slips and trips, each fall depositing us onto a catwalk that would lead us to another ascent, another fall, and so on.

Back in 1966, when I was 13 years old, I followed behind Denny and his girlfriend as he walked her home from school. They were cute...Denny's lanky form beside her petite one. When he leaned down and spoke soft words, she giggled. I studied them from 10 steps behind.

When their relationship fizzled, I was a ready understudy. Mine became the small figure alongside Denny's towering one. We always lingered on the wooden footbridge spanning Wildwood Creek and threw stones at objects below. Denny, an avid baseball player, never missed. I watched in adoration.

Suspended on that ancient structure, we first held hands, kissed, and eventually murmured, *"I love you"*—stepping-stone words that bridged us to an uncertain universe of passion and commitment. But that first year we basked in unspoiled bliss.

People got used to seeing me balanced on the banana seat of Denny's

Stingray bicycle as he pedaled me home after ballgames. What brilliant romantic invented banana seats, and where are those loveseats today?

We lived in a world of two, so we invented our own social events. New Year's Eve we piled on layers of clothing, grabbed a thermos of hot chocolate, and skimmed down legendary sledding hills at Wildwood Park. Moonlight on snow illuminated our love of nature and cemented our relationship.

Water connected us in summertime. I spent my J.C. Penney paychecks on a tiny sailboat that we strapped to Denny's Firebird. His earnings provided gas. We drove 25 miles to Lake Wapello and hoisted our sail, allowing wind to pull us across the water for picnics in a grassy clearing. Kissing distracted us once, a near tragedy occurring when our charcoal grill set fire to fall prairie grass. Romance went up in smoke, as we scrambled for lemonade and lake water to douse the flames. Our lives were laced together with such disasters.

Later, in separate colleges, we agreed to date around. But when I went out with other guys, Denny's face appeared ghostlike between us. A letter or a phone call would pitch us back together. How do you sever the lifeline that defines your place in the world? After seven years of dating, we felt we should either let go or commit. Six weeks later we were married.

Our 1974 wedding was a hippie dreamscape, the aisle a strip of freshly cut grass in the pastor's backyard. I wore white cotton and a crown of daisies on my long straight hair. Harp strings twinkled "Claire de Lune," and acoustic guitar accompanied folksy love songs. When it was time to kiss, we missed our marks, my lips lining up perfectly...with Denny's armpit. We looked like awkward distant cousins. *"And the bride may now kiss the groom's shoulder...."* Why didn't we rehearse "The Kiss?" We tumbled into an abyss of unpreparedness together.

Even our honeymoon was unplanned. After two long days in the Firebird, we rented a crude cabin just across the Canadian border. Rainy Lake's glassy surface reflected a groom in an old fishing boat towing his waterskiing bride. When purple-black clouds appeared, that groom sped full throttle back to shore. We hurriedly tied the boat, laughing and reaching our cabin just as storm clouds cracked open. We had our first married fight that night when Denny chose to watch TV.

Everything seemed different after that. I felt underappreciated, and Denny felt crowded. Happiness was always just beyond reach. Our honeymoon cloud lingered. Had marriage changed passion into something else?

We forged on for a decade. Friends of ours were to be married on our 10th anniversary. Running late to the wedding, we settled in a back pew. I studied the bride and groom as I dabbed at my eyes. *All that beauty, all that passion, all that love—to be tainted by the two simple words, "I do."* If forced to give an account of our own marriage, I would have said, "Maybe we're just falling out of love."

But at the very moment the groom placed a ring upon the bride's finger, Denny reached for *my* finger and slipped a tiny gold band upon it. Seven diamonds reflected their sparkle to my eyes. And I fell in love again—just like that.

We had not decided whether we would have children. But as we approached our mid-thirties, we agreed to let God choose. When I became pregnant, Denny and I formed a remarkable partnership. The pregnancy showed early signs of trouble, and we held each other up.

In my 28th week, I awoke with a still, hard lump where our baby lay inside me. We rushed to the hospital where our dream became a nightmare; instead of a baby shower, we would plan a funeral. Denny swabbed my forehead and rubbed my legs through 24 hours of hopeless labor, and I gave birth to our first child. We peered through tears as the nurse placed a tiny girl with pink stocking cap into my arms. Her skin was silky and cold. We buried Anne's ashes on a hill at the family farm.

Just 364 days later, a doctor presented us with a perfect baby boy. Two years passed, and another daughter was born but did not breathe. They whisked her away in a helicopter, a nurse's hand pumping air into her tiny lungs. An angel must have hovered above, for this little girl survived, bringing us profound joy. For several years, blue skies pushed the clouds away.

As time passed, Denny and I drifted apart again. Those days, I secretly envied Tom and Kathy, about our age, a couple I observed walking together, holding hands, constantly smiling and laughing. They moved away, and I saw Tom a couple years later at a café. "How's Kathy?" I asked.

"Oh, didn't you hear? We divorced." Tom's answer echoed in my heart.

Denny and I soldiered on. We tumbled through a cavern of diapers and doctors, careers and vacations, games and recitals, fast food and birthday cakes. Memories melded us together. Years later, Denny assembled videos for high school graduation parties, and I witnessed the roles we had played: two sets of hands reaching and serving, lifting and comforting. A pair of dark circles held up my eyes. We had not focused on our marriage, but it fell in and flowed along with the cluttered current that is parenthood. We were blessed.

When my father became terminally ill in 2003, I asked my husband, "Do you think Dad should live with us?" Our home was chaotic with teenagers, but Denny answered without hesitation, "Rex should use our bedroom, since it's close to the bathroom." I fell in love with my groom again, this time for good.

After Dad's funeral, we toiled side-by-side as we emptied my parents' house. I reflected on the girl I once was, riding home balanced on Denny's bike seat. Back then, we'd inhabited a carefree world of two.

Now that my parents have passed, the kids grown, our world is small once again. We finally have time to tend to the marriage. We find ourselves no longer centering a bicycle, but teetering on a slippery roof.

How did we survive 38 years and end up on this icy roof? Did love or grace lift us up out of harm's way? Perhaps after all our falls, we've simply gotten good at climbing back up. Or maybe it really doesn't matter at this point. For from here we can finally see our tale of marital mishaps fade as a love story falls softly onto the page.

KRISTI PAXTON lives in the woods with husband, Denny, and dog, Ziggy. A substitute teacher, she writes freelance features for the *Waterloo-Cedar Falls Courier*. When not at work, she is kayaking, bicycling, reading, beachcombing, or drinking coffee. A perfect day includes all.

**kristipaxton.wordpress.com**

# Don't Miss...

# F'ALLING *in love* WITH YOU

41 REAL LOVE STORIES GUARANTEED FOR A SMILE

COMPILED & EDITED BY
RAMONA TUCKER & JENNIFER WESSNER

Surprised by Love...

Where did you first meet the person you fell in love with? The person with whom you could be totally you? Or do you still dream of that magical moment, when you know you're in head-over-heels, dancing-in-the-rain kind of love?

Fall in love again...or for the first time...with 41 of the sweetest real-life love stories collected from across the globe. They're guaranteed to make you smile.

*For other great love stories:*
**www.oaktara.com**

# About the Compilers/Editors

**RAMONA CRAMER TUCKER** has been on the cutting-edge of publishing for nearly 30 years, in a wide variety of positions, including: Senior Editor, Tyndale House Publishers; Editorial Director, Harold Shaw Publishers (now WaterBrook); Editor, *Today's Christian Woman* magazine and Executive Editor, *Virtue* magazine (Christianity Today, International); as a freelance writer/editor/project development specialist for Simon & Schuster, Random House, Viking-Penguin, Zondervan, Nelson, Baker/Revell, InterVarsity, Howard, David C. Cook, Barbour, HarperCollins, Summerside/Guideposts, and other publishers. She is Cofounder and Editorial Director of OakTara and Adjunct Faculty for the English Department at Wheaton College.

**JENNIFER WESSNER**, a Wheaton College graduate with a B.A. in Literature and History and a former journalist, now works as OakTara Publisher's Social Networking Director.

Waterford, Virginia

**www.oaktara.com**
- *Fresh, new authors. Leading-edge established authors.*
- *Inspirational fiction in nearly every genre, from suspense to romance*
- *Mind-stretching, heart-transforming, life-inspiring nonfiction*